RESOURCE BOOKS FOR TEACHERS

series editor

ALAN MALEY

EXAM CLASSES

Peter May

Oxford University Press 1996

Oxford University Press
Walton Street, Oxford OX2 6DP

Oxford New York
Athens Auckland Bangkok Bogota Bombay
Buenos Aires Calcutta Cape Town Dar es Salaam
Delhi Florence Hong Kong Istanbul Karachi
Kuala Lumpur Madras Madrid Melbourne
Mexico City Nairobi Paris Singapore
Taipei Tokyo Toronto

and associated companies in
Berlin Ibadan

Oxford and *Oxford English*
are trade marks of Oxford University Press

ISBN 0 19 437208 1

© Oxford University Press 1996

Photocopying

Set by Wyvern Typesetting Ltd., Bristol

Printed in Hong Kong

Acknowledgements

The publishers and author thank the following for their kind permission to reproduce extracts from works for which they hold the copyright.

The BBC for extracts from Ceefax (page 306, 1 April 1995) and from 'The Modern Sherlock Holmes' (BBC World Service, 25 Jan 1991), reproduced with permission.

Educational Testing Service for portions of TOEFL test directions, reprinted by permission of the copyright owner. The test questions and any other testing information are provided in their entirety by Oxford University Press. No endorsement of this publication by Educational Testing Service should be inferred.

Diana Fried-Booth and Oxford University Press for extracts from *PET Practice Tests*.

The *Guardian* for an extract from 'Flying with the fret set' by Melanie Phillips, *The Guardian Weekly*, reproduced with permission © The *Guardian*.

Hodder and Stoughton for an extract from *A Perfect Spy* by John Le Carré by permission.

The *Independent* for an extract adapted from 'Downhill all the way' by Jeremy Hart.

The *Linguist* for extracts from 'Teaching Languages Holistically' by M. Lawlor, by permission.

Oxford University Press for definitions from the *Oxford Advanced Learner's Dictionary* (5th edition).

Oxford University Press and Diana Fried-Booth for permission to reproduce an exercise from *PET Practice Tests* © Oxford University Press.

Penguin Books and Colin Smythe Ltd on behalf of the estate of J. C. Medley for an extract from 'Untilled Field' by G. Moore from *The Penguin Book of Irish Short Stories*.

Stena Line for an extract taken from a brochure with permission.

Times Newspapers Limited for extracts from 'Giving the game away' by Rachel Cooke (*The Sunday Times* Style 11 Dec 1994) and from 'A new deck of cards' by Paul Nuki and Nick Gardner *The Sunday Times* News Review 23 April 1995, © Times Newspapers Limited, 1996.

Trinity College London for an extract from an exam paper (note: candidates taking the Intermediate examination will not get the words provided in this book).

University of Cambridge Local Examinations Syndicate for extracts from examination questions and rubrics.

University of Michigan for an extract from MELAB 1994–5 Information Bulletin and Registration Form.

University of Oxford Delegacy of Local Examinations for permission to reproduce extracts from examinations.

Contents

The author and series editor

Peter May is a freelance teacher, teacher trainer, writer, and translator based in Brussels, Belgium. He taught in Spain for fifteen years, including six years with the British Council at the British Institute for Young Learners in Madrid. There he worked as a teacher of CFE and CPE classes, co-ordinator, and Cambridge oral examiner. He also helped to run a number of summer courses in the UK. More recently he has taught at the Centre de Langues in Luxembourg and the University of Trier in Germany, and has helped individual students prepare for other exams including PET, CAE, IELTS, the International Baccalaureate, and TOEFL. He has written numerous articles on teaching for exam classes, and three books: *The Complete Proficiency Practice Tests 1* and *2* and *First Choice for Proficiency* (Heinemann). He is married with two young sons.

Alan Maley worked for The British Council from 1962 to 1988, serving as English Language Officer in Yugoslavia, Ghana, Italy, France, and China, and as Regional Representative in South India (Madras). From 1988 to 1993 he was Director-General of the Bell Educational Trust, Cambridge. He is currently Senior Fellow in the Department of English Language and Literature of the National University of Singapore. Among his publications are *Literature*, in this series, *Beyond Words*, *Sounds Interesting*, *Sounds Intriguing*, *Words*, *Variations on a Theme*, and *Drama Techniques in Language Learning* (all with Alan Duff), *The Mind's Eye* (with Françoise Grellet and Alan Duff), *Learning to Listen* and *Poem into Poem* (with Sandra Moulding), and *Short and Sweet*. He is also Series Editor for the Oxford Supplementary Skills series.

Foreword

Exams—the thing we all love to hate! Examinations have been part and parcel of language teaching all along and will doubtless continue to be so. Everyone hates them yet, at the same time, we all recognize their importance for measuring our achievement against our personal goals, for proving our worth in the academic stakes, for improving our career prospects. They also have the potential to change educational practices through their powerful 'washback effect' on teaching and learning. In short, they cannot be ignored.

This book attempts to address the difficult problem of how to teach 'exam classes' without losing sight of the need to teach the language too. All too often, examination books prove to be no more than tactical guides to techniques for passing the exam. It is as if it were possible to learn the exam rather than learning the language. By contrast, the activities set out here are as valid for language learning as for testing.

An important strength of the book is its attempt to demystify the examination by taking students behind the scenes and making them a party to the sorts of decisions made by those who design test items, thus building self-confidence.

Many of the activities use the textual material of examinations, especially the rubrics, as their raw material, making 'examination language' part of the language learning (and examination preparation) process. This too is designed to ensure complete familiarity with the special language of rubrics and in this way to develop complete confidence in handling such kinds of text.

The activities have been carefully designed to cover the item types used in a wide range of current tests and examinations. Item types and activities are cross-referenced throughout. The teacher of the examination class is therefore provided with a flexible inventory of activity types which can be further built upon in the light of particular needs. No one teaching examination classes will want to be without it!

Alan Maley

Introduction

Who this book is for

This book is for teachers whose students are preparing for a public examination, either in their own country or abroad. The exam will probably be in the elementary to advanced level range and may be oral or written in nature, or both. It might consist of more traditional, accuracy-based tasks like essay writing and multiple-choice questions or be based on more practical, 'real world' tasks such as responding to an advertisement, and proof-reading. Some students may be taking the exam for academic or professional reasons—to qualify for entry to college or university, to get a job or promotion. Others may be doing so for purely personal reasons—because they enjoy studying English or because they want to get extra qualifications. Younger learners may be taking the exam because their parents or teachers want them to.

You, the teacher, may have taught exam preparation classes before, or you may be new to this kind of teaching. You will probably be concerned that your students are prepared as well as they possibly can be for the examination; and you will want to make your lessons motivating, varied, and relevant.

The activities in this book have been designed to prepare students for the kinds of task that they are likely to face when taking English-language exams set by the main British, European, and American examining boards, including the Cambridge First Certificate in English (1996 Revised), the Certificate of Proficiency in English, the Certificate in Advanced English, the (1995 Revised) TOEFL, TSE, and TWE, the Oxford-Arels Examinations, the Trinity College London Grade Examinations and the International Baccalaureate.

It may be years before your students actually become candidates, but if their aims are both to pass the exam and improve their language skills, this book should have lots to offer both learners and teacher. It can be used to supplement either a coursebook, a range of skills books, or your own material.

One of the main aims is to demystify the exam. This book sets out techniques which show students how exam questions are meant to be answered—for example 1.6 'Reading the instructions'; how item-writers and examiners think—for example 2.13 'Avoiding multiple-choice traps' and 3.2 'Essay marks'; even—in a number of activities such as 5.7 'Writing dual-choice questions'—how to write their own exam items for their partners.

What makes exam classes different?

Many teachers feel that working with exam classes has certain advantages. Firstly, students usually share the same aim: to pass the exam. Their needs are largely similar and a sense of common purpose frequently develops, motivating them to work hard both inside and outside the classroom.

Students often find that the lessons resemble the kind of exam-oriented accuracy-based learning which they may be familiar with. Hard work soon leads to evidence of progress which can be measured regularly by both student and teacher, thus providing further encouragement.

Syllabus design, too, is easier, as the exam requirements are clearly laid down, and different papers or sections of the exam provide neat divisions for timetabling and lesson planning.

There can, however, be disadvantages. In some cases the level of the exam can be so high that few of the class have much chance of passing it, and there may well be varying levels within a class. Students sometimes meet unfamiliar task types in the exam, for example having to talk to another candidate in the oral when they have done little or no pair-work practice in class, or being told to write a formal letter in a set time when they have not practised writing any kind of letter in English. And sometimes students are just too young for the exam they are expected to take.

But perhaps the biggest problem is the potentially negative effect which the exam can have on the exam class. An exam which requires mainly written answers may tend to produce a course which neglects speaking skills, and accuracy may be valued much more highly than fluency. In this case lessons imitate the exam. Texts are followed by multiple-choice questions or turned into cloze tests. Isolated and often contrived sentences test knowledge of individual words and structures. Letters on boring topics have to be written to anonymous readers who are never going to write back anyway. Errors are to be avoided at all cost.

All this can lead to a course consisting far more of testing than of teaching. This book helps to rectify these problems by giving teachers and students an insight into how exams work.

Teaching exam classes

The choice of exam

Most examining boards now accept that the nature of the exams they set will inevitably influence what happens in the classroom. Some now test real-world abilities in a more natural way:

practice for them should help the learner develop genuinely useful language skills. Where these exams are more appropriate to the learners' needs teachers should be encouraging demand for them, but whatever the exam you will want to do all you possibly can to help your students to build their language skills and pass it.

Language input and practice

Exam techniques have to be built on a solid foundation of language skills. Students cannot handle a difficult exam course without a thorough grounding in reading, writing, listening, and speaking. They will also need to be able to recognize and use a wide range of structures and vocabulary: help with these areas is provided in activities such as 4.10, 'Grammar search', and 2.2, 'Word search'. See also other titles in the Resource Books for Teachers series such as *Vocabulary*, by John Morgan and Mario Rinvolucri.

One great difficulty your students are likely to have if they do not live in an English-speaking country is lack of exposure to authentic language. Nowadays most exams use a wide range of texts that are either authentic or at least similar to those which a student might expect to see or hear outside the classroom. Learners will benefit from all the help you can give them with using English-language libraries, press, radio, TV, information via computer, associations, and personal contacts. Activities in the book which encourage the use of these sources include 3.8, 3.15, and 5.5.

Doing plenty of homework is essential for most of the exams listed on pages 159–63 and private study should be regarded as an integral part of the learning process. Some exam practice exercises, especially essays and reading comprehension, simply have to be done at home if there is to be time in class for other activities. Other useful homework assignments include:

– studying a grammar point for the next lesson;
– revising new vocabulary;
– preparing a talk;
– self-correction of written work;
– preparing for a progress test;
– reading set books;
– finding new sources of authentic language.

Practice tests

Practice tests and past papers certainly have an important role as a means of familiarizing students with the exam format—activity 4.1, for example, helps with this—and practising timing, as suggested in 1.10. But over-use can be boring for students, the exam certificate but also in the improvement in their general level of English and the development of specific skills. At the start of the year you should ask the class to think about how their personal aims can be achieved through these three forms of success, then get them to consider which aspects of their English they will have to work on most (1.1). At various stages of the year you might like to ask them to reflect on which of their aims are already achievable, and remind them to think long-term, well beyond the exam. How will they use their language skills in the real world? You might want to remind the class that passing an exam is not the only measure of success in learning. Fulfilling their potential can be just as rewarding. For more learner-training activities, see Chapter 1 'Strategies'.

Dealing with different levels within the class

There are bound to be varying levels within the class but the differences do not have to be permanent. It is fascinating—and extremely rewarding—to watch conscientious, hard-working students catching up with the higher-flyers. They can be helped by avoiding difficult exam-style exercises that produce depressingly low scores—some cloze tests, for example—until they have been shown how to do them (see 4.2) and have practised with simplified versions.

Correction is best done gently with weaker learners. We should avoid covering written work in red ink and concentrate at first just on errors which impede communication rather than every minor mistake (it is best to tell the class at the start of the course of our intention to do this). Errors should not be regarded as 'failure' but as a chance for students to learn from their mistakes, to work out language rules and patterns for themselves. A similar approach should be adopted with spoken language: students may well have to demonstrate fluency under pressure in the interview, so their confidence needs building up. Decide on a correction code for all written work. This could include, for example: G=Grammar, V=Vocabulary, WO=Word Order, Sp=Spelling, P=Punctuation. When checking work, write the appropriate letter at the end of the line containing this type of error. Students then have to find the mistake for themselves and self-correct, rather than passively notice there has been a correction—or worse still, just be given a mark for the work. Don't forget to check their self-correction. (See also 4.4.)

Teachers need to be flexible: you can suggest lower minimum-word limits for weaker students when they write essays, bearing in mind that the homework you set may be taking them much longer to do. And you can help them while they are working by giving them encouragement and perhaps a few clues. With quicker or more skilled students, an extra related task can be done while they work or when they finish. For example, if the class are practising letter-writing the stronger students can be given extra points to include, or asked to write a brief reply.

An exam classes bank

Building up a bank of reference and classroom material greatly assists with lesson-planning and activity preparation—especially if a number of teachers can work on it together. It also means the material you prepare is used again and again, and can be modified according to classroom results. The bank could be divided up as follows:

1 Information on the exam: syllabus, specifications, regulations, dates, local recognition, surveys of results, any planned changes, current set books, examiners' notes, marking scales, etc.

2 Past papers: these should be filed in chronological order, with a note where any changes to the syllabus, format, or rubrics occurred. Papers from other exams can often be useful, particularly their listening and reading texts. Most exam boards (see pages 159–63) will supply past papers or sample tests at a cost which should be affordable for most institutions. A list of text types, topics, and situations which regularly appear in the exam would also be useful, and can help with preparation for activities such as 5.14 and 6.8.

3 Practice tests: at least one book of tests is essential, not least for use in conjunction with this book (though not always for the purpose for which the exam tasks were intended). Teacher's books or with-key edition marking schemes are useful, as long as the scoring criteria are exactly the same as in the exam (it is also advisable to check that the tests faithfully reproduce the format of the exam questions). Lists of the latest practice test books (and coursebooks) are not given in the Bibliography on page 164 as they rapidly become outdated. The easiest way to find details is by looking at the publishers' catalogues.

4 Texts: It is a good idea to collect plenty of interesting (to the students, that is) texts which are similar in length, language type, and topic area to those used in the target exam. Newspaper and magazine cuttings—including pictures—should be clearly marked with their source and date. A collection of short, interesting items on audio cassette

taken from the radio is also useful. Keep photos containing a variety of people, objects, or places. They should not be too dissimilar from each other, for example they could be of people at a sports or cultural event, cars in the street, or buildings in a particular city. These can be used in activities like 6.5. Photos of people of about the same age range and background as your students are particularly good for comparing and contrasting, and would be useful for activity 6.2. Try to ensure they are set in work, social, or sporting contexts that reflect the students' personalities and interests. The students' own books may be a good source of pictures like these, but useful photos can also be found in EFL books of just about any level.

5 Students' work: of particular use in conjunction with this book is a good stock of written work—essays, open-ended answers, summaries, etc.—and recordings of students' spoken English, preferably in the context of mock oral exams. The aim is to use them with other classes of the same level, perhaps in a subsequent course or year. In each case the piece of work should be labelled with the level and age of the student, plus the date, teacher's name, and target exam. It might also be useful, later on, when the student takes the exam, to note the date and result.

6 Activities: when you have done one of the activities in this book—or prepared one of your own—it makes sense to keep any materials you used, a record of how it went, and suggestions, either for your own future use or for other teachers. Perhaps open a file for each activity and classify according to the sections in this book or the parts of the exam your students are going to take. Each time it is used, the date, class, and number of students should be noted and comments made, for example: How long did it in fact take? How did local conditions affect it? Did it involve all the students or did some look left out? Did they look as though they were learning? Which stages went best? Will you repeat the activity and if so when? Can you think of ways to adapt it to your teaching—and the students' learning—circumstances? You may want to ask the class what they think, perhaps by means of a questionnaire—and pass on any new ideas to your colleagues. The writer of this book would be pleased to hear about them, too!

How to use this book

How the book is organized

The activities are divided into six chapters: 1: 'Strategies', 2: 'Reading', 3: 'Writing', 4: 'Grammar', 5: 'Listening' and 6: 'Speaking'. The first chapter focuses on the learner, while chapters 2–6 will in many cases correspond to parts—or papers—of the exam. At the beginning of each chapter there is a short introduction which describes the activities it contains and at the end are answers to questions in the exam tasks.

There is no need to follow the sequence of the chapters as they are printed in the book, although you may prefer to start with some activities from the 'Strategies' chapter so that students are thinking about the exam, the practice materials, and their own learning right from the beginning.

Some of the activities at the beginning of each chapter are designed to be used at the start of the course, often as a form of introduction to the exam tasks and the skills required to deal with them, for example 2.1, 3.1, and 4.1. In general those nearer the beginning of the chapter are intended more for use early on, though with classes who are expecting traditional exam practice it might be advisable to introduce them gradually. In many cases the activities are grouped according to task type, for example multiple-choice questions in 2.12, 2.13, and 2.14. A few of the activities near the end of the chapter should be left until later in the course. This is clearly the case where the aim is revision—for example 1.12—but it may also be the best thing to do where the activity requires the kind of familiarity with the exam tasks which only usually comes as the exam itself approaches, as in the cases of 6.13 and 6.14.

Although the most obviously useful activities will be those aimed at the exam your class are taking, do not ignore the others. For example, their test of spoken English may not have a section called, or consisting of, 'Situations', but activity 6.11 is an excellent preparation for other oral tasks such as role-plays and simulations. And remember that although the book is divided into skills areas, many of the activities actually develop more than one skill, for example 2.10 (reading and writing), 3.6 (writing and speaking), and 6.12 (listening, writing, and speaking).

At the back of the book there is an index of the main task types covered, so that you can easily find all the activities which focus on the type of question you want to work on. Remember, though, that many activities are useful for a range of task types within one area such as Reading Comprehension, while a few (1.1, for example) are not aimed at any in particular. You may also sometimes need to adapt activities slightly to suit the exam your students are preparing for, or for your particular students.

An Examinations appendix outlines some of the most popular exams. More detailed information about them can be found in the books listed in the Bibliography, which also contains a list of materials which can be used with the activities in this book.

How each activity is organized

Each activity is organized under similar headings.

Level
This shows the lowest language ability level normally required for the activity to be successful. Many activities will be equally useful for classes above this minimum, so most state a level such as 'Intermediate' followed by 'and above'. The terms used—elementary, lower-intermediate, intermediate, upper-intermediate, and advanced—correspond approximately to Carroll and West's *ESU Framework* scales 3, 4, 5, 6, and 7 respectively.

Aims
This indicates the exam task type and the skill(s) the activity is aimed at. Many of the examining boards use similar task types, so an activity is often relevant to a number of exams (see the Index of Tasks on page 166). Where an activity practises more than one skill—reading and writing, for example—it is grouped under 'Writing' if its main aim is preparation for the part of the exam which tests writing skills.

Time
This shows the average amount of class time the activity should take.

Preparation
This explains what materials you will need and any steps you should take before the activity begins. It is best to check the details under this heading well before the lesson in which you plan to do the activity.

Examples of how to prepare the activity may be given in the text or under a separate subheading.

Procedure

The stages of the activity are explained on a step-by-step basis, as in a condensed lesson plan.

Example

Where appropriate, an example of how the activity works in practice is given. It is often shown in the context of the relevant exam task. A key to questions in the examples is given at the end of each chapter.

Follow-up

Sometimes an extra stage can be added to the procedure, possibly in a subsequent lesson or for homework.

Variation

Some activities can be done in a slightly different way by changing one or more of the stages in Procedure, often to cater for higher or lower levels. Others can be varied if certain materials are available, while a few can be transferred to another skills area: reading comprehension tasks to listening comprehension, for example. Sometimes more than one variation is possible and of course your own teaching circumstances may make others advisable.

Comments

Further advice and comments on the activity are included under this heading.

1 Strategies

This chapter consists of activities designed to raise awareness of exam questions and materials, increase learner independence, and help students to tackle exam papers, thus providing them with confidence-building strategies to improve their language performance at home, in the class, and in the exam room. Although the activities are applicable to any exam, some of them do have particular relevance to certain skills areas. This is the case of 1.1 (speaking), 1.2 (speaking), 1.3 (grammar), 1.6 (reading), 1.7 (listening), 1.8 (speaking), and 1.11 (writing).

Several of the activities have a significant learner training element in that they help students find effective learning strategies suited to their own way of studying. Activity 1.1 introduces student self-assessment from the beginning of the course, encouraging learning by making students think about what they can already do and how they can do more. In 1.2 and 1.3 they start thinking about the exam itself, both in terms of how difficult they feel each of its component parts is and which preparation activities they would enjoy doing. This should provide useful information for planning the course. 1.4 highlights learner diaries, an ongoing self-assessment technique which enables students to keep a record of their progress that they can refer back to. 1.11 is an activity for later in the course, which encourages students to think about repeated errors and to look for them actively in their work without being prompted. If they do this regularly, by the time they sit the exam it should have become an exam strategy too.

The second group of activities highlights the exam papers, encouraging students to concentrate on the contents so that they know exactly what they are supposed to do when exam practice begins. Activities 1.5, 1.6, and 1.7 (see also 3.9) focus on the all-important instructions, ensuring that students understanding the language of the rubrics, what the implications are, and what kinds of task-type they tend to go with. In 1.8 the emphasis is on the texts used in exams, encouraging students to use reading strategies to make a quick and efficient assessment of materials they encounter in spoken or written papers.

The final group is concerned with strategies for success in the exam itself. Activity 1.9 forces students to think about the exam tips given in published materials, all too often ignored or not fully understood but here the subject of active study. The aim of 1.10 is to make students aware of how many marks are allocated per section and how this should affect the amount of time they spend on each, especially when the exam paper contains various task-types. Activity 1.12 is designed for use just before the exam, encouraging students to find the source of the exam advice for themselves.

1.1 Learner aims

LEVEL	**Elementary and above**
AIMS	**To develop and reinforce a positive attitude towards the course; to practise oral decision-making**
TIME	**45 minutes**
PREPARATION	None
PROCEDURE	

1 Groups brainstorm all the ways the course will be useful to them in the future. They note down aims that can be achieved by: (a) passing the exam; (b) improving their level of English in general; (c) developing specific skills. For example:

a – Do a higher exam in English.
  – Work as an interpreter or translator.
  – Go to university in my own country.
  – Teach English.
  – Go to a foreign university.
  – Work abroad or for a foreign firm.

b – Travel abroad for professional reasons.
  – Understand textbooks in English.
  – Meet people from other cultures.
  – Visit other countries for pleasure.
  – Read English literature.
  – Live in another country.

c – Reading reports.
  – Writing formal letters.
  – Note-taking in lectures.
  – Proof-reading.
  – Summary writing.
  – Being interviewed in English.

2 Each student makes a list of personal aims.

3 They ask themselves these questions and write the answers:

  – Which can you do now?

  – Which should you be able to do when you have finished the course?

  – Which skills do you need to improve in order to achieve your aims?

FOLLOW-UP   Later in the course, get the class to review their aims in each category, as well as their answers to the three questions. What changes have there been? Why? Then, at the end of the course, encourage them to think about which of their aims they have achieved, and how.

COMMENTS   Students are more likely to achieve aims if they set them for themselves rather than being told what they should be. It is also important that students realize that their aims need not and should not be limited to passing the exam—as well as the fact that (b) and (c) in stage 1 above do not necessarily depend on (a).

1.2 Likes and dislikes

LEVEL   Elementary and above

AIMS   To encourage students to think about the exam and how to prepare for it

TIME   45 minutes

PREPARATION   None

PROCEDURE   1 At the start of the course, tell the class that it would be interesting for you to know what they feel are the hardest parts of the exam, and also what kinds of activity they would like to do to prepare for it.

2 For homework, tell the class to go carefully through a set of past papers or a complete practice test, grading each section for difficulty—as it seems to them—on a scale from 1 (the lowest) to 10. In the Speaking paper of Cambridge First Certificate, for example, a student might put:

Part 1 (socializing and giving personal information)—3/10
Part 2 (talking about pictures)—7/10
Part 3 (talking to another candidate)—4/10
Part 4 (talking to another candidate and an examiner)—6/10

3 In the next lesson, discuss the findings as a class. Then choose one exam paper and write on the board a list of classroom activities associated with it, for example:

   pronunciation exercises   role-plays   simulations
   debates   games   giving a prepared talk
   reading a text aloud   problem-solving   telling jokes
   talking about a short text   discussing a book
   prioritizing   brainstorming

Ask the class which activities would them prepare for which parts of the paper.

4 In pairs they decide which they enjoy, which they don't, and which they think are most useful as exam preparation.

5 Discuss as a class and keep a note of the findings. Having plenty of information on what students find difficult, for example, can make diagnostic tests unnecessary.

FOLLOW-UP

Repeat the activity later in the course. Perhaps organize a class survey: choose two or three students to go around the class and ask the others their opinions, in what way they have changed, and why. They report back to the class, who discuss the findings—in particular the reasons for any changes.

1.3 Easy or difficult?

LEVEL

Lower-intermediate and above

AIMS

To encourage self assessment and oral exchange of opinions

TIME

45 minutes

PREPARATION

1 This activity is best done at the beginning of the course, before the class has done any exam practice.

2 Ensure everyone can see examples of all the question-types likely to appear in a paper of the exam they are going to take.

PROCEDURE

1 Explain to the class that they will be thinking about their own strengths and weaknesses, talking to other people in the class about theirs and—later in the course—seeing whether their feelings about the different task types change.

2 As a class, discuss each part of the paper in turn.

3 The students draw up—in their notebooks—a table similar to the one below. Make sure that they understand the names of the types of question, and that every section of the paper is included.

Example

What do you feel about each type of question in the Use of English paper?

	Easy	Average	Difficult
Multiple-choice cloze			
Open cloze			
Key word transformations			
Error correction			
Word formation			

(*Cambridge First Certificate in English*, Revised 1996)

4 They say how they feel about each by ticking the appropriate box.

5 They do a survey of class feelings. Groups (in larger classes) or individuals (in small classes) are allocated a question-type and they ask everyone else for their opinions on it, noting down the results.

6 Go through the findings as a class.

7 Tell them to keep the tables and survey results for comparison purposes when they repeat the activity later in the course.

8 If time allows, repeat with another paper of the exam.

FOLLOW-UP 1

In a subsequent lesson, when the students have practised doing all the question-types, they compare their scores to their self-assessment in the table. Which did they overestimate or underestimate their ability to do?

FOLLOW-UP 2

Further into the course they repeat stages 2–6 above and compare the results. What changes have there been? Why?

COMMENTS

Apart from its learner training element and start-of-course ice breaking, this activity should provide some useful feedback on class wants and needs. Keep the results: when planning practice activities or revision, proportionately more class time should be allocated to those questions types which the students themselves regard as difficult.

1.4 Exam class diaries

LEVEL

Elementary and above

AIMS

To encourage learners to think about their own progress

TIME

15 minutes, then 5–10 minutes per lesson

PREPARATION

Tell the class to bring a new notebook to the lesson.

PROCEDURE

1 At the beginning of the lesson, put some suitable diary main headings on the board or OHP, for example: *Things I enjoyed; Problems I had; What I learnt; Marks I got.* Tell the class to think about them during the lesson.

2 At the end of the lesson elicit points under each heading and put them on the board.

3 Working alone, students fill in their own details under each heading.

Example
Things I enjoyed
Interesting text in the reading comprehension (space travel). Group work: planning. Reading the transcript of the listening. Dictation!

Problems I had
Timing in grammar exercises, especially the gap fill. Too many new words in the listening. To remember the word for 'étoile'.

What I learnt
Vocabulary: rocket, to launch, gravity, light years, solar system, to land, spacesuit. Pronunciation of 'height': /haɪt/. One 'o' in 'lose'. 'It depends on something'. Don't spend more than 10 minutes on the gap fill. Don't try to understand every word in the listening.

Marks I got
Grammar: 16/30. Listening: 4/10. Reading comprehension: 7/10. Dictation: 5/10.

FOLLOW-UP 1

At the end of each lesson, allow five to ten minutes for students to fill in their diary entry for the day.

FOLLOW-UP 2

At the end of the term, students use the notes in their diaries to write brief reports on their work—including self-assessed marks for the term's work—and give them to you. Compare them with your reports and marks. Discuss any significant discrepancies with the individual students.

COMMENTS

A diary record of how they felt and what they did provides students with useful data to reflect on, especially when they want to know why they are doing well or badly. They should not take too much notice of sudden drastic changes in the marks they are given, but ought to see a gradual overall improvement during the course—assuming, naturally, that marks are awarded on constant criteria.

1.5 The vocabulary of instructions

LEVEL   **Elementary and above**

AIMS   **To understand and practise using important rubric vocabulary**

TIME   **20 minutes**

PREPARATION   **1** At the beginning of the course, make a list of key words from the exam instructions (written or spoken).

2 On the board or OHP, or on a worksheet, create two columns headed 'expressions' and 'definitions'. Write in the expressions and jumble the definitions.

Example

expressions	definitions
true (adj)	square enclosed space on the page
cross out (v)	group of words with a subject and verb
fill in (v)	mark which shows something is wrong
box (n)	not to include
underline (v)	mark which shows something is correct
missing (adj)	add what is necessary to complete
tick (UK) check (US) (n)	remove by drawing a line through
phrase (n)	correct
gap (n)	not present
sentence (n)	draw a line under
leave out (v)	group of words without a verb
cross (n)	empty space between two words

PROCEDURE   **1** In groups or individually, students match each word to its definition. Check that everyone has the right answers written down and ask them to draw examples where appropriate, for instance a tick (check) in a box.

2 Put everyone into pairs—student A/student B—and make sure they have a large piece of paper ready.

3 Prompt all the student As to write exam-style instructions using words from the 'expressions' column. In each case the Bs respond in writing, showing whether they have understood the instructions. For example:

You say:	Student A: write a sentence with a *gap* in it.
Student A writes:	April is the month of the year.
You say:	Student B: *fill in* the gap with one word.
Student B writes:	April is the fourth month of the year.

4 Look at their work and check for complete accuracy.

5 The class scan past papers for any other rubric words they don't know, check them with you, and add them to the list on the worksheet. This could be done for homework.

Examples

1 Student A: write a *phrase*.
Student B: *cross out* the phrase.

2 Student A: draw *a box*.
Student B: put *a cross* in the box.

3 Student A: write a short *sentence*.
Student B: *underline* the sentence.

4 Student A: write something *true* about your partner.
Student B: put *a tick* next to that sentence if it is true.

5 Student A: write a sentence and *leave out* a word.
Student B: write a word which *fits* the sentence.

COMMENTS Although most students assimilate everything in the instructions after a certain amount of exam practice, some may not do themselves justice through an initial failure to understand essential words.

1.6 Reading the instructions

LEVEL **Elementary and above**

AIMS **To encourage careful reading of exam instructions**

TIME **Variable; this activity is particularly useful at the start of the course**

PREPARATION Choose a number of standard instructions used in the target exam. Treat them as reading comprehension texts and devise a number of true/false or multiple-choice questions for instructions which might be confusing or unfamiliar to students.

PROCEDURE 1 Stress the need to follow exam instructions to the letter.

2 Students answer the questions you have devised and then check with their partners.

3 As a class, study any difficulties that arise. Focus on the relevance of the wording to actual exam questions, for instance the importance of choosing answers according to what the text says rather than what students might already know about the subject.

Example

PART 4

You are going to read some information about some British cities.
For questions **24–33,** choose from the cities (**A–H**). Some of the cities may be chosen more than once. When more than one answer is required, these may be given in any order. There is an example at the beginning (**O**).
For questions 34 and 35, choose the answer (**A, B, C** or **D**) which you think fits best according to the text.
Mark your answers **on the separate answer sheet**.

(Cambridge First Certificate in English, Revised 1996)

Questions	True	False
1 Part 4 has two different types of question.		
2 You should write down the names of the cities.		
3 Each city can only be chosen once.		
4 If two cities are possible, put the better answer first.		
5 In question 34 you can put more than one answer.		
6 You must write your answers in the boxes on this question paper.		

VARIATION 1   For higher levels, a *Not Stated* (*NS*) column could be added:

	True	False	NS
7 You must only do Part 4 when you have finished Part 3.			
8 You will lose marks if you put a wrong answer.			

VARIATION 2   At lower levels it may be advisable first to focus on any difficult words used in the instructions.

1.7 Identifying the tasks

LEVEL   Lower-intermediate and above

AIMS   To focus on exam instructions and link them to text type

TIME   30 minutes; this activity is best done early in the course

PREPARATION   1 Make a list of listening comprehension rubrics from several examinations including the one your students are preparing for.

2 Make sure everyone has access to plenty of past papers from the target exam.

PROCEDURE

1 Working alone or in pairs, students study the list of rubrics and the past papers. Below the appropriate rubric on the list, they note down the serial numbers (or dates), part or question numbers, and question types of the exam tasks which have the same—or very similar—instructions.

2 As a class, go through the findings. Using the exam tasks as examples, ensure that everyone understands exactly what the rubrics specify.

3 In pairs, they classify the exam tasks according to text type, for example: formal interview, story, advertisement, telephone message, informal conversation, series of speakers, public announcement, news report.

4 They match the text types to the rubrics.

5 Discuss the findings as a class.

Example

1 You will hear people talking in a number of different situations. Choose the best answer, **A, B,** or **C.**
0187/4, 1st part; 3-option multiple choice; short informal conversations.

2 After you hear a question, read the four possible answers in your test book and choose the best answer.
67545, part A; 4-option multiple choice; short dialogues.

3 Listen and fill in the missing information on the form below. Some of it has been filled in for you.
0164/4, 1st part; write on form; descriptions of objects.

4 Look at the picture in your booklet. Listen to the route Mrs Jones describes and draw a line to show it on the picture. Also mark the bank with a cross.
AP65, question 6; write on map; directions.

5 A phrase or sentence will be spoken with special emphasis. Choose the answer that tells you what the speaker would say next.
9856, questions 7–9; 3-option multiple choice; phrase or short sentence.

6 For each of the questions tick one box to show whether the statement is true or false.
0340/4, 3rd part; tick 1 of 2 boxes; traffic news.

VARIATION

This activity can also be used with reading comprehension rubrics and texts.

COMMENTS   Emphasize the importance of becoming completely familiar with the instructions likely in the exam, and point out that certain rubrics tend to go with certain text types, for example:

fill in the gaps below—*recorded telephone messages*

put a tick in the box you think is the most suitable—*descriptions of four objects*

put them in the order in which you hear them—*extracts of different people talking.*

1.8 Understanding the materials

LEVEL   **Intermediate and above**

AIMS   **To develop rapid text comprehension and inferring skills in oral examinations; to improve oral fluency**

TIME   **40 minutes**

PREPARATION   Choose three different oral exam practice tasks such as role-plays, information gaps, or discussions which involve the use of written texts. Prepare a range of questions about the first two.

PROCEDURE   1 Write your first set of questions on the board or OHP. The class study the first text and answer the questions. Elicit more questions and answers about the same text.

2 Write your second set of questions. In pairs, students study the second text. They ask each other about it, using your questions and any others they can think of. When they have finished, elicit these questions and put them on the board.

3 For the third text they work alone, asking themselves about it and writing down both their questions and their answers. Check what they have written.

4 They do the exam task, using the text from stage 3.

COMMENTS   This activity aims to get students into the habit of asking themselves questions about these texts. Repeat it whenever they are practising this kind of task, perhaps setting a time limit of a minute or two when they are working alone.

1.9 *Dos* and *Don't*s

LEVEL

Lower-intermediate and above

AIMS

To improve exam skills through intensive reading and oral decision-making

TIME

20 minutes +

PREPARATION

Choose a list of exam tips from a coursebook (or better still, make your own) for a given question-type. Leave out or rephrase any which are too obviously affirmative or negative sentences (for example *Don't leave any sentences incomplete*), as the correct answer can be given mechanically without any thought about the advice given.

Example

Discuss your answers to the six questions below. Give reasons and, if possible, examples from your personal experience.

Are you a traveller or a tourist?

When you are abroad, do you usually:

1a sample as much as you can of the local food?
 b try to eat the same things as at home?

2a take an interest in events in the country where you are?
 b prefer to keep up with the news from your own country?

3a make an effort to learn some of the local language?
 b hope that everyone you meet speaks your language?

4a read a book about the history and culture of the country you are in?
 b read a cheap novel you picked up at the station or airport?

5a visit places where foreigners like you don't usually go?
 b go only where there will be lots of people from your country?

6a enjoy being in a culture where they do things differently?
 b laugh at the way they do things abroad?

Questions
 – What is this kind of text called?
 – Where is it probably taken from?
 – Is the language used formal, informal, or neutral?
 – Who would probably read it?
 – Which verb tense is used? Why?
 – What is the apparent purpose of the text?
 – What is implied by the text?
 – What might people be thinking while they read it?
 – What usually follows this kind of text? Why?
 – How might people feel after they have read it?

Photocopiable © Oxford University Press

PROCEDURE

1 Focus attention on the list of exam tips you have chosen. In pairs, the students decide which are *Do*s and which are *Don't*s.

Sample exam tips

Writing a narrative essay

Which of these things should you do and which should you not do?

In each case put Do *or* Don't *at the beginning of the sentence.*

1 _____ highlight the key words in the title on the question paper.

2 _____ write about something different if you don't like the title.

3 _____ spend time planning your essay.

4 _____ write more than the specified number of words.

5 _____ tell the story in the present simple.

6 _____ think about mistakes you have made in the past.

7 _____ leave a gap if you can't think of a word.

8 _____ write a draft of your essay and then copy it out.

9 _____ put an alternative in brackets if you think you might have made a mistake.

10 _____ leave ten minutes at the end to check your work.

Photocopiable © Oxford University Press

---

2 Discuss as a class. In each case elicit reasons for the advice and ask what would happen if a candidate did not follow it.

3 Pairs or groups suggest more *Do*s and *Don't*s for the same type of question.

VARIATION

Instead of deciding which techniques to use, students sequence them. This example focuses on multiple-choice text comprehension questions.

Put these steps in the best order.

a read each question

b decide which is the right answer

c study the relevant part of the text carefully

d if you're not sure, eliminate the impossible ones and guess

e quickly read the whole text

f mark the part(s) of the text which relate to the answer

g look at the alternative answers given

Photocopiable © Oxford University Press

1.10 Question timing

LEVEL

Elementary and above

AIMS

To think about the marking scheme and about timing in exams

TIME

60 minutes +

PREPARATION

1 Find out how many marks are given for each part of the grammar paper. For some exams these are indicated in the teacher's book accompanying past papers, but it is best to check for variations from year to year.

2 Ensure that everyone has access to a typical exam paper together with its marking scheme.

PROCEDURE

1 Students look at the exam paper and draw up a table like the one in the example, working out for themselves the number of questions and marks per section.

2 They decide how many minutes they should allocate to each part of the paper, allowing time for (a) reading the general instructions at the beginning, (b) coming back to any questions they were getting stuck on, and (c) a final check through at the end. Remind them to spend less time on low-scoring questions. Try to reach a consensus on approximate timings so that when they do exam practice there is a class dynamic of completing sections, turning pages, and finishing the paper at approximately the same time.

3 Say what time they will be starting to write. Check that everyone can see a reliable clock, or (younger students love this) synchronize watches.

4 Get the class to write alongside each part of the paper the time when they should have finished it.

5 They start to answer the questions. You may wish to remind them from time to time which section they should have reached.

6 Check the answers, give marks, and find out which parts of the paper held people up. Elicit reasons and solutions.

Example

Time: 90 minutes	Total marks: 56		
Section	*No. of questions*	*Marks*	*Minutes*
Error correction	12	12	16
Sentence completion	6	8	11
Sentence transformation	10	18	24
Filling one-word gaps	10	10	13
Expanding notes	4	8	11

Allow for reading instructions, unfinished questions, and checking: about 15 minutes.

(Cambridge Advanced Certificate in English)

COMMENTS

1 Remind the class how essential it is to finish all the questions on the exam paper, and point out that to achieve accurate timing they should make a plan and practise following it.

2 To save class time, choose just one part of the exam and give the class the generally agreed time to complete it in. Doing this regularly should get students used to working against the clock—and greatly reduce the risk of panic when they actually get into the exam room.

3 This activity can also be used with reading comprehension and vocabulary papers which use a number of task types. Point out that in order to offset the random guessing effect, true/false and yes/no comprehension questions may carry only half the marks of others.

1.11 Top ten mistakes

LEVEL

Elementary and above

AIMS

To encourage the habit of checking for mistakes

TIME

30 minutes, plus a few minutes in subsequent lessons

PREPARATION

This activity is best done when students have built up a fairly large file of corrected work.

PROCEDURE

1 Tell the class that there are likely to be certain errors they make again and again, and that eliminating these can considerably improve the standard of their work.

2 At home, students go through their work and make up a 'league table' of their ten most common errors.

3 In the next lesson, pairs compare their lists and report back to the class. You can note the findings for remedial and/or revision work.

4 Tell students to keep their list handy whenever they are doing a writing task, checking their work for each of those mistakes when they have finished.

5 Repeat a few months later. Students (and you) can compare lists then and now.

Example

  1 prepositions: *at*, *in*, and *on*
  2 when to put the definite article
  3 present simple following *when, after*, etc.
  4 *being* or *been*
  5 where to put commas
  6 capital letters
  7 verbs followed by *-ing* or infinitive
  8 *there* or *their*
  9 *both . . . and* (not *and . . . and*)
  10 its and it's

VARIATION

This activity is also suitable for spoken language. Suggest that students record themselves when they are speaking in English and give each other the tape to note down the main errors. When they have plenty of data to work from they draw up a list similar to the one above.

1.12 Revision questions

LEVEL

Intermediate and above

AIMS

To practise writing and answering revision questions about exam strategies

TIME

60 minutes

PREPARATION

Look at the advice in the coursebook or exam practice book on exam strategies. On a worksheet or OHP transparency make a list of 12 questions with a note of the page where the answer to each can be found.

PROCEDURE

1 Elicit the answers to two of the questions. Students check the answers for themselves by looking in the book. Make sure they have the right answers.

Example

a Question: *In what order must you do the questions?*
(coursebook page 58)

Text: You can do the questions in any order you wish, but it may be best to do the simpler ones first. Make sure you don't get stuck and fail to reach questions you could have done easily.

Answer: *Start with the easier ones.*

b Question: *When you write your answers, can you use words from the text?*
(coursebook page 149)

Text: Use your own words where you can, but there is no harm in using individual words from the text.

Answer: *Yes, but not too many.*

2 In pairs, students ask each other the remaining ten questions and then check with the book. Go through the answers when they have finished.

3 Focus on a page in the book where an answer was found. Elicit more questions on exam strategies and ask the rest of the class to answer them.

4 The class study the other pages mentioned on the worksheet. Each student thinks of one question (two or three in smaller classes). They write it on a piece of paper—together with its answer and the page reference—and hand it to you. Check for accuracy and make a note of any advice that has been misunderstood.

5 Read out the good examples; elicit the answers. In each case give the page reference and get the class to look for the answer, then check.

6 Revise any misunderstood advice.

COMMENTS

This activity is best done towards the end of the course, when the students are thoroughly familiar with the coursebook. It can also be used with grammar, vocabulary, phonology, and the main skills areas.

Answers

1.6	1 T	2 F	3 F	4 F	5 F	6 F	7 NS	8 NS
1.9	1 e	2 a	3 c	4 f	5 g	6 b	7 d

2 Reading

The activities in this chapter will help prepare students for examination papers such as 'Reading Comprehension', 'Reading', and 'Reading and Writing'.

Most examining boards expect candidates to be able to read and understand the kinds of texts they will meet in everyday life, ranging, for example, from signs, notices, and simple texts at elementary levels to messages, letters, newspaper/magazine articles, reports, advertisements, informational material, and academic or literary texts at more advanced levels. For lower-level exams, therefore, students will need to show their ability to skim factual texts for gist and scan them for specific information. At intermediate levels they could be asked to identify the text type, recognize attitudes and emotions expressed by the writer, say what the writer's purpose is, and understand text structure. At higher levels they may be required to decide whether a test is based on fact or opinion, to select information and use it to perform a task, infer meaning from context, appreciate style, and recognize attitudes or emotions implied by the text. Some exams, such as TOEFL and Cambridge CPE, also test understanding of individual words as they are used in the text.

The difficulties for students will of course vary according to the kind of exam and the level, but there are some problems that most candidates will face. First they will need to be familiar with many different kinds of text and sources, which may not be easily available if they are studying in countries where English is a foreign language. For suggestions on this see the 'Exam classes bank' section of the Introduction. Another problem is the speed at which candidates have to read and understand text, which at higher levels can be real time, that is, the time taken in a real-world situation. This can be made easier by training students to predict text content (2.6), to summarize paragraphs as they read (2.3), and not to pore over every word (2.1).

Perhaps the most daunting aspect of texts, however, is the vocabulary load. We can help here by using practice materials as sources of lexical input (2.2, 2.9, 2.10, 2.15), encouraging dictionary use to build vocabulary (2.15), and developing word-attack skills such as identifying false cognates (see 4.14) and studying affixes (see 4.13). Students at intermediate and higher levels will encounter other challenges such as understanding and identifying cohesive devices (2.8), appreciating stylistic features (2.11), and focusing on the writer's purpose, attitudes, and feelings (2.4).

Many of the activities (2.1, 2.2, 2.4, 2.6, 2.8, 2.9, 2.10, 2.11, 2.13, 2.14, 2.15) are designed for students taking virtually any of the major exams. Most of the task types commonly found in exams are covered, for example multiple-choice (2.12, 2.13, 2.14) as used in many of the UCLES exams, TOEFL, MELAB, Trinity, and the ICC; true/false or yes/no (2.13, see 5.7), also in many UCLES exams; reference word questions (2.8), as in Cambridge CPE, the International Baccalaureate (IB) and IELTS; information transfer (2.5), in the Oxford-Arels Higher, the IB, Cambridge CAE, and CCSE; and free-response questions (2.7), in Cambridge CPE, the Oxford-Arels exams, the IB, and Pitman.

In information transfer and free-response questions writing skills are also needed. This is taken a stage further in activity 2.10, where the passage is used as a model for text writing. The increasingly popular technique of multiple matching—as used in Cambridge FCE and CAE, and IELTS—is featured in 2.3 and 2.16 (see also 1.6), while matching words and phrases—as in the IB—is included in 2.9. Open cloze (gap-fill) texts—of the kind found in most of the UCLES exams, MELAB, Trinity, and the ICC—are dealt with in 2.1 and the type of multiple-choice cloze now used in FCE is the focus of 2.12. Cloze tests are also covered in the Grammar chapter (4.1, 4.2, 4.3, 4.11, 4.12). Other task types include rewriting in-context expressions (see 2.9), found in Cambridge CPE and the Oxford-Arels Higher, and predicting the continuation of a text (2.6) in TOEFL.

Further activities in other sections with a component aimed at reading comprehension include the focus on instructions in 1.6, reading for main points in 3.5, reading for specific language in 3.8, and reading for gist in 3.9. Reading texts are also used as writing models in 3.5 and 3.8, and for recognition of register in 3.12.

2.1 Skimming texts with gaps

LEVEL	**Lower-intermediate and above**
AIMS	**To encourage the reading of cloze texts for gist**
TIME	**40 minutes**
PREPARATION	Choose a suitable cloze test and write some short questions about it on the board or OHP. These questions should focus on the text type, the gist and the main points—and not depend directly on the missing words for their answers.

PROCEDURE

1 Make sure that everyone understands the questions you have written up, then hand out the text.

2 Tell students they have a few minutes to read it but they must not attempt to fill in any gaps. Instead they are to note down answers to your questions.

3 As a class, discuss the answers.

4 Students fill in the gaps.

5 Check the answers (see the end of the chapter for an answer key).

Example

Fill each of the numbered blanks in the following passage. Use only one word in each space.

One evening I went to a sports centre for some exercise.

(1) .... I was changing afterwards, I dropped (2) .... wallet down the back of a radiator. Obviously, it (3) .... important for me to get it out, but it (4) .... to be very difficult. In the end I managed to get it (5) .... the help of a hockey stick (6) .... had found. This (7) .... have taken me half an hour, and when I had finished, I discovered that everyone (8) .... had gone. The building was empty and most of the lights (9) .... been turned off. I made my (10) .... down a gloomy passage and came to the door. To my horror it was securely locked.

Questions

a What kind of text is this?   b What is a *wallet*?

c What happened to it?   d How did she get it back?

e Why was the building empty?   f Where did she go then?

g What did she discover?   h What would be a good title for the text?

FOLLOW-UP

Repeat whenever the class do a cloze, but get the class to think up more and more of the questions—so that by the time they take the exam they automatically ask themselves questions about the text. This should help them form an overall impression and provide context for the missing words.

VARIATION

Make your own cloze tests. Choose texts of up to 250 words each and leave a maximum of 20 gaps per text, the length of the text and the number of gaps varying according to level. In order to provide a lead-in, you may wish to leave the first few lines complete. Make copies for students or prepare OHP transparencies of each text, both with and without the gaps. Ask the class questions as above. When the students have answered they compare with the original text to check their comprehension. They may be surprised at how much they have understood of an incomplete text, and you can point out that the same is often true of a text containing difficult words. Finally, they fill in the gaps.

2.2 Word search

LEVEL

Lower-intermediate and above

AIMS

To build vocabulary through extensive reading

TIME

20–30 minutes

PREPARATION

None

PROCEDURE

1 Make a list of useful words which come up while the class are doing reading comprehension, transformation, word formation, cloze, or other tests of vocabulary. Nouns, verbs, and adjectives connected to the topic of the current (or next) lesson might be of particular interest. Try also to include some 'structural' words which often cause difficulties, such as *despite*, *hardly*, and *whether*.

2 As a homework task, students read whatever they like and find as many examples as they can of the words on the list. (Dictionary entries and sentences they have written do not count!)

3 They bring the sources—books, magazines, or whatever—to the next lesson.

4 In groups they check each other's examples and report back to the class on which student has found the most.

5 Some of the best examples can be dictated (by the students who found them) to the rest of the class for inclusion in their vocabulary notebooks.

VARIATION	Students look for specified structures in their reading. These could range, for example, from basic passives or comparative forms such as (not) as . . . as at lower levels, to the subjunctive or conditionals without if in more advanced classes.

COMMENTS	Remind the class that seeing new expressions in more than one context makes them easier both to store and to locate in the long-term memory.

2.3 Matching headings to paragraphs

LEVEL	**Lower-intermediate and above**

AIMS	**To practise multiple matching by summarizing paragraphs**

TIME	**45 minutes**

PREPARATION	1 Select two multiple matching (choosing headings for paragraphs) exam papers and ensure there are enough copies of both for the class.

2 For the first paper, think of a phrase or short sentence to summarize the content of each paragraph.

3 Write your sentences on the board, OHP, or test paper and number them according to the paragraphs they refer to.

PROCEDURE	1 Tell the class to study the list of paragraph headings in the exam paper and to match them to the paragraph summary sentences you have written.

2 Students check their answers by reading the text.

3 Go through the answers as a class.

4 Focus on the second exam paper but tell students to cover up the list of headings. This time they must read the text and then write the paragraph summary sentences for themselves. It may be best for them to work in pairs or groups. Monitor their progress.

5 Students match their sentences to the headings.

6 Check their answers (see key at end of chapter) and suggest they follow steps 4 and 5 whenever they do this task type.

Example
*You are going to read a magazine article about car theft. Choose the most suitable heading from the list **A–I** for each part (**1–7**) of the article. There is one extra heading which you do not need to use. There is an example at the beginning (**0**). Mark your answers **on the separate answer sheet**.*

AN EXPENSIVE BUSINESS

As car crime soars, DAVID ROWLANDS and CHRISTOPHER JONES plot the rise of car theft in Britain.

0	I

A million motorists leave their cars full up with petrol and with the keys in the ignition every day.

1	

The vehicles are sitting in petrol stations while drivers pay for their fuel. The Automobile Association (AA) has discovered that cars are left unattended for an average three minutes— and sometimes considerably longer—as drivers buy drinks, sweets, cigarettes, and other consumer items—and then pay at the cash till. With payment by credit card more and more common, it is not unusual for a driver to be out of his car for as long as six minutes, providing the car thief with a golden opportunity.

2	

In an exclusive AA survey, carried out at a busy garage on a main road out of London, 300 motorists were questioned over three days of the holiday period. Twenty-four per cent admitted that they 'always' or 'sometimes' leave the keys in their cars. This means that nationwide, a million cars daily become easy targets for the opportunist thief.

3	

For more than ten years there has been a bigger rise in car crime than in most other types of crime. An average of more than two cars a minute are broken into, vandalized or stolen in the UK. Car crime accounts for almost a third of all reported offences with no signs that the trend is slowing down.

4	

Although there are highly professional criminals involved in car theft, almost 90 per cent of car crime is committed by the opportunist. Amateur thieves are aided by our own carelessness. When AA engineers surveyed one town centre car park last year, ten per cent of the cars checked were unlocked, a figure backed by a Home Office national survey that found 12 per cent of drivers sometimes left their cars unlocked. The AA recommends locking up whenever you leave the car—for however short a period. A partially open sunroof or window is a further come-on to thieves.

5	

There are many other traps to avoid. The Home Office has found little awareness among drivers about safe parking. Most motorists questioned made no effort to avoid parking in quiet spots away from street lights—just the places thieves love. The AA advises drivers to park in places with people around—thieves don't like audiences.

6	

Leaving valuables in view is an invitation to the criminal. A Manchester Probationary Service research project, which interviewed almost 100 car thieves last year, found many would investigate a coat thrown on a seat. Never leave any documents showing your home address in the car. If you have a garage, use it and lock it—a garaged car is at substantially less risk.

7	

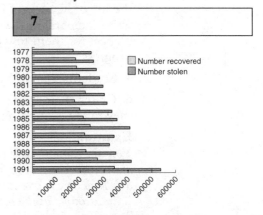

A Watch where you park
B Car crime increase
C Large car parks are safer
D Will you get it back?
E Three minutes is all it takes

F One in ten invites thieves
G Take it with you
H A million cars are at risk
I Take the keys with you

Teacher's paragraph summary sentences:

1 Thieves don't need much time.
2 Too many drivers take a chance.
3 It's a huge and growing problem.
4 Don't make it easy for criminals.
5 Be careful when you leave the car.
6 Don't leave it in the car.
7 You might never see your car again.

COMMENTS

You could suggest to students that they extend this technique to texts in general: doing a quick mental summary of each part as they go along is an excellent way of improving comprehension and reading efficiency.

VARIATION

This activity can easily be modified for use with task types which require students to match summary sentences with paragraphs.

1 Think of headings for the paragraphs and get the class to match them to the summary sentences on the exam paper.

2 Proceed as in the main activity, except that students must write their own paragraph headings in step 4 and match them to the summary sentences at step 5.

2.4 Responding to texts

LEVEL

Elementary and above

AIMS

To encourage students to evaluate and respond to reading texts

TIME

30 minutes

PREPARATION

1 Draw up a list of questions designed to elicit a personal response to reading texts.

2 Choose an exam reading comprehension text that you think will be of interest to your students. It could be accompanied by multiple-choice, open-ended, or other kinds of question.

Example

> **a** What did you feel after you read the text? Why?
>
> **b** Did you find it easy to read? Why/why not?
>
> **c** What kind of person do you think the writer is? Why?
>
> **d** Would you like to read more about the topic? If so, what?
>
> **e** What is the purpose of the text? Is it achieved? How?
>
> **f** Do you agree with what the writer says? Why/why not?
>
> **g** Is the writer impartial or biased in what he or she says?
>
> **h** Do you find the writer's arguments convincing? Why/why not?
>
> **i** Is there anything in the text that you don't understand?
>
> **j** What have you learnt from the text?

Photocopiable © Oxford University Press

PROCEDURE

1 Point out to the students that meaning can become much clearer if they think about why and how the writer wrote a text, and about the effect it has on them as readers.

2 Hand out copies of your list of questions, or write them up on the board/OHP. Check that everyone understands them.

3 Working individually, and without attempting to answer any of the exam questions, the students read the text.

4 The students select some of the questions on the list—the choice will depend on the nature of the text and the level of the class—and write down their answers.

5 Students compare their responses with partners or others in a group.

6 Ask the class how they feel about the text: there may be some useful feedback on the kinds of text they find motivating.

FOLLOW-UP

For homework students answer the exam questions in the usual way.

VARIATION

This technique can also be used with listening comprehension texts. On the first time of hearing, students ignore the exam questions and concentrate on the personal response questions. The recording is then played the usual once or twice—depending on the target exam—and the students answer these questions.

COMMENTS

Tell students to get into the habit of asking themselves some of these questions every time they read a text. This should help them see comprehension passages as authentic language written by real people, and encourage learners to react much in the same way as they do when they read a text in their first language.

2.5 From text to chart

LEVEL	Upper-intermediate and above
AIMS	To practise information transfer and writing headings
TIME	20 minutes
PREPARATION	1 Find a suitable text and make a chart of the information it contains (see the example below). Put short column headings in the form of questions about the text topic in the top row, and answers in the bottom row. Then delete some of the column headings.

2 Gap the parts of the text that correspond to the answers in the chart.

3 Make copies or an OHP transparency of both the chart and the text, as well as the originals.

Example

Using the information from the leaflet The Traveller's Guide to Health, *complete the missing data on the chart below in note form.*

(extract)

....	....	....	Vaccination certificate needed?	....
Most parts of the world, but especially in conditions of poor hygiene and sanitation	(3) *Contaminated food or water*	(4) *Immunoglobulin shortly before travel*	No	Take scrupulous care over food and drink

(25) As we soar and plunge, the shaking gets worse. The cabin staff start rumbling their trolleys down the aisle. I keep my eyes fixed on the procession like a talisman. They don't even *look* worried. They're even smiling. They're even looking bored. I take the cup of coffee with shaking hand and spill it. The cabin staff smile (30) blandly and look the other way.

Having defied all natural laws and got up there, I can't believe we'll stay up. So I talk compulsively to anyone who happens to being sitting nearby. Habitual reserve and prohibitions on chatting up strange men disintegrate at 35,000 feet. The trouble (35) is, the other passengers are usually as terrified as I am.

32. The paragraphs following the passage most likely discuss which of the following?
(A) How she feels as the plane lands.
(B) How to make air travel safer.
(C) What she does at her destination.
(D) What happens on the return flight.

The Guardian

VARIATION

Students work in pairs with a text from their coursebook or a newspaper/magazine article. Student A reads the whole text while B reads only the first part of it. Student B predicts subsequent paragraphs as A gradually moves the card down the page, commenting on the accuracy of B's predictions. They then discuss an imaginary continuation of the text.

2.7 Free-response questions

LEVEL

Upper-intermediate and above

AIMS

To practise writing free-response reading comprehension questions and answers

TIME

30 minutes

PREPARATION

1 Ensure the class are familiar with the format of this task type. Go through a few questions, in each case isolating the corresponding part(s) of the reading text.

2 Set more questions for the class to write their answers to. Elicit the answers and then set a few more. This time put the answers and marking scheme on the board or OHP and give students practice at marking each other's work. Point out that they do not usually need to repeat the question in their answer.

3 Choose a suitable text, draw up questions, and make two copies. Remove some of the questions from the first copy and write in the answers. Underline the relevant part(s) of the text and number them according to the question they answer.

Now take the second copy and do the same, but with different questions and sections of the text underlined.

4 Make a class set of copies labelled 'Student A' or 'Student B'.

Example

Student A (extract)

There is only one thing that can be done quickly to get to the root (1) of the problem of the old and the cold. That is to reduce the burden of their fuel costs. The elderly are dying because their heating is too expensive and because, for too much of the year, most of us manage to forget about the problem. We only become indignant as the pensioners start to collapse (3). We ought to be more consistent. Yet the central responsibility is collective . . .

1 Q _____?

   A *The basic cause.*

2 Q What is the only immediate solution?

   A _____.

3 Q _____?

   A *We only think about it in winter, by which time it is too late.*

4 Q What does 'Yet' mean in the last sentence?

   A _____.

Student B (extract)

There is only one thing that can be done quickly to get to the root of the problem of the old and the cold. That is to reduce the burden of their fuel costs (2). The elderly are dying because their heating is too expensive and because, for much of the year, most of us manage to forget about the problem. We only become indignant as the pensioners start to collapse. We ought to be more consistent. Yet (4) the central responsibility is collective . . .

1 Q What does 'root' mean in the first sentence?

   A _____.

2 Q _____?

   A *Make it cheaper for them to heat their homes.*

3 Q What, in general, do we do about the problem?

   A _____.

4 Q _____?

   A *But.*

PROCEDURE

1 Students study the text and write in the missing questions.

2 Without showing their worksheets, students ask their partners the questions they have written. They make a note of the answers they are given.

3 Still in pairs, the students discuss their questions and answers.

4 They compare both with the originals on the worksheets.

VARIATION

With more advanced classes, the numbers against the relevant parts of the text can be omitted.

2.8 What does 'it' refer to?

LEVEL

Lower-intermediate and above

AIMS

To practice reference word questions

TIME

45 minutes

PREPARATION

None

PROCEDURE

1 On the board or OHP, highlight some of the reference words—the use of *this*, *that*, *it* etc. to avoid repetition—in one or more short texts appropriate to the level of the class. Point out that most refer backwards, but that forward reference is also possible.

2 Underline a few more and get the class to say what they refer to, for example:

Bianca and Ricky have a major row. But does it mean the end or will she forgive him?

3 The class study a variety of texts in their coursebook, exam papers and, at higher levels, press articles, noting down all the reference words they can find. This could be set as a homework task.

4 As a class, draw up a list of reference words, for example:

Backward: this   that   the   these   those   he
she   it   him   her   they   them   mine
yours   his   hers   its   ours   theirs   some
many   one   another   such   each   every
other   either   neither   both   so (I think so)
not (I hope not)   then   there   in this way
the above   the former   the latter

Forward: below   the following   this   these

Elicit spoken examples of the words in context.

5 In pairs, students study a variety of texts—possibly including their own (corrected) written work—and ask each other 'What does ____ refer to?' questions.

<table>
<tr><td>FOLLOW-UP</td><td>Students use correction fluid to blank out the reference words of a text and swap with their partners, who do the same with a different text. They fill in the gaps.</td></tr>
</table>

2.9 In other words

<table>
<tr><td>LEVEL</td><td>Intermediate and above</td></tr>
<tr><td>AIMS</td><td>To practise paraphrasing and build vocabulary</td></tr>
<tr><td>TIME</td><td>30 minutes</td></tr>
<tr><td>PREPARATION</td><td>1 Choose a text of more than 200 words similar to that used in the reading comprehension part of the exam. The text should contain a reasonable number of new expressions, but not very long or highly complex sentences.

2 Pick out about half a dozen words or phrases, underline or highlight them, and write underneath the text a list—in random order—of their meanings. A dictionary may be useful here.

3 Select some more expressions from the text and make a second, separate list of their meanings—but do not highlight them in the text.</td></tr>
<tr><td>PROCEDURE</td><td>1 To introduce the activity, choose one or two expressions from the text and ask the students to give you another word or phrase with similar meanings.

2 Each student matches the meanings to the underlined expressions in the text. Check and perhaps focus on the connotations of words—in the example below, for example: *lurk* (something sinister) *scuttle* (small animals, possibly escaping) not normally associated with *hide and wait* and *run*. Remind students that true synonyms are rare in English.

3 Students scan the text for equivalents to expressions in the second list. If they are taking too long, give paragraph, sentence, or line reference clues.

4 By this stage most of the more difficult expressions should have been studied. In pairs, students make their own lists of meanings for more words and phrases (possibly using their dictionaries) and get their partners to find equivalents in the text. You may wish to check these definitions before they show them to their partners, especially with lower levels.</td></tr>
</table>

Example

a *Read the text carefully and match these expressions to the underlined words and phrases.*

circle   covered in vegetation for many years   dominate
hide and wait   dries out the ground   run   noise

There is no escape from the ferocity of the afternoon sun. The shade from the stunted oak trees only serves to trap the heat shimmering up from the cracked, yellowish ground. The dense jara bushes have lost their brilliant white blossom; the multicoloured wild flowers which so briefly carpeted the hills and valleys have dried. When summer arrives, the pitiless sun quickly blasts the moisture out of the earth. The bone-dry air is odourless, seemingly sterile; the only sound the distant rumble of traffic. Nothing, it seems, would choose to live here. The long-overgrown trenches from the Civil War—this was the front line for 3 years—are something people would rather forget.

But above, in a vast blue sky that stretches to the snow-tipped peaks of Guadarrama and Gredos, birds of prey wheel and swoop. At ground level, too, the hunters are around. Tread softly and you may spot a fox, a six-foot snake, or a huge luminous-green lizard lying in wait. Under stones and logs lurk short-tempered white scorpions and poisonous giant centipedes. Rabbits scuttle across the narrow footpaths; the occasional stag leaps across the fence from the neighbouring royal game reserve. It is the Iberian wild boar, though, that rule La Quinta. Chunky and fearless, when disturbed they will attack the biggest dog— and anyone with it.

b *Find words and phrases in the text which have similar meanings to these expressions.*

where the fighting took place   jumps
land used for hunting   nearby   undersized
apparently   see   irritable

c *Work in pairs. Without telling your partner which they are, choose six words or phrases from the text and make a list of similar expressions. See if he or she can match them correctly.*

2.10 Using text vocabulary

LEVEL Intermediate and above

AIMS To practise using reading texts as a model for writing

TIME 60 minutes

PREPARATION 1 Select a reading comprehension text on a subject which would make a suitable topic for the writing section of the exam.

2 Taking into account the level of the class, pick out the words and expressions in the text that could be useful in the writing task.

PROCEDURE 1 Explain to the class that they are going to use certain features of a reading text as a model for their own writing.

2 Put the class into pairs: student A and student B in each case.

3 Give half the vocabulary items you have chosen to the As and the other half to the Bs.

4 The students read the text and use contextual clues to determine the meanings of the words on their own list. Dictionaries can be used for any really difficult expressions.

5 As a class, discuss the topic and identify language features of the text, such as verb tenses, linking words, and register.

6 Students do the exam task.

7 Set a writing task on a similar topic. Students should use as many of the words on their list as they can, underlining them as they write.

8 In the next lesson they read each other's completed work and explain the meaning of the underlined words, if necessary referring back to the reading comprehension to look at them in another context.

Example

Giving the game away

• In the Manner of the Word

Written down, In the Manner of the Word can sound a little boring. It isn't. It can be one of the best games ever. All that is required are a good few drinks beforehand, and the requisite number of show-offs. The best version is played something like this. The players form teams of two. One team leaves the room to think of an adverb—timidly, hysterically, or whatever. The rest of the party then gives them a situation—presenting Top Of The Pops, putting on make-up—which one of them must act out *in the manner of the word*. The group's aim is to guess what the word is.

• The Quotation Game

This is for literary types. One person, the leader, copies out an entry from a dictionary of quotations, telling the rest of the group only what its theme is. The piece of paper is then screwed up into a ball and thrown into a hat. Everybody else has to write their own 'mock' quotation on the same theme, before putting it in the hat too. The leader then reads each quotation out in turn. The group must identify the real quotation and, if possible, its author. Points can be picked up along the way by those whose own quotation is mistaken for the real thing.

• I Have Never

This is a deceptively simple party game. One guest stands up and announces something they have never done: 'I have never... flown in a helicopter.' Anybody else who has never flown in a helicopter stands up too. Everybody must be honest. If nobody stands up, then you have won. But more fun is to be had in seeing who remains seated. Predictably, this quickly becomes *very* rude.

The Sunday Times

Language: present simple, sequencing words, modals, conditionals.

Possible expressions:

Student A	Student B
guest	fun
in turn	identify
points	mistaken
players	version
act out	teams
aim	guess

Writing task: *You have been asked to contribute a paragraph to a magazine article about party games in different parts of the world. Describe a game which is popular in your country.*

2.11 Between the lines

LEVEL Advanced

AIMS To practise answering comprehension questions on stylistic features

TIME 60 minutes

PREPARATION 1 Choose a reading comprehension text which contains examples of (for instance) irony, exaggeration, understatement, euphemism, metaphor, or puns.

2 Write extra questions on the board, using the same format (multiple-choice, open-ended, etc.) as the exam task. These questions should elicit the technique used by the writer.

PROCEDURE 1 The class quickly read the text for an overall impression.

2 Students look at the text again and answer, orally, the questions you have set.

3 In pairs, they identify all the examples of the technique that are used in the text.

4 Where they can, the students rephrase the examples.

5 Students make a list of more examples of the technique that they have heard or read, possibly translating them from their first language, and report back to the class.

6 They do the exam task.

Example

1 What is the purpose of this text? What is the significance of the date?

2 What do many of the verbs have in common? Why has the writer done this?

306	CEEFAX 306	Sat 1 April	11:59/00

BBC Football: Craven Cottage set to sink?

Fulham officials have been plunged into despair by the news that their famous Craven Cottage ground is sinking into the River Thames.

The 3rd division outfit, more used to plugging holes in their defence, have splashed out on 50,000 sand bags to stop the slide.

Furious club chairman Jimmy Hill said: 'I don't know who leaked this . . . the calls have been flooding in. We get our heads above water financially, then this happens. It's ridiculous. The pitch is going under water but I'll keep my chin up.'

BBC Ceefax

3 Find all the words associated with 'water'.

4 In each case, give another expression—not necessarily associated with water—that means the same.

5 Can you think of any other 'water' puns?

6 Answer the exam questions.

COMMENTS   Point out to the class that even where exam questions focus only on facts, stylistic features can make the text difficult to understand fully.

2.12 Previewing texts

LEVEL   **Lower-intermediate and above**

AIMS   **To practise multiple-choice cloze questions and predicting**

TIME   **30–40 minutes**

PREPARATION   1 Choose a reading comprehension text that has a rather heavy vocabulary load and make a list of about six key words or phrases (checking that they are not also the focus of questions in the exam task).

2 Write the clauses or sentences containing these words on a worksheet or OHP transparency, but leave blanks for the key words themselves.

3 Underneath each extract, put three or four multiple-choice options including the original word. Where possible, make the distractors useful vocabulary items too.

PROCEDURE   1 Show the class the multiple-choice questions but not the whole text. They should be allowed to use dictionaries to answer them as this is not a testing activity.

2 Check the answers and the meaning of the distractors.

3 Students predict the context of the reading comprehension text from the multiple-choice questions they have studied.

4 They study the complete text and do the exam task in the usual way.

Example

> *Choose the right word from A–D to fill the gap.*
>
> **1** . . . while over 26 million ___ saw the Christmas episode, which is a record for TV in this country . . .
>   A watchers   B viewers   C spectators   D onlookers
>
> **2** The storylines, some critics say, tend to ___ too much on love triangles . . .
>   A trust   B base   C rely   D establish
>
> **3** . . . using a plane crash to get ___ of characters who have overstayed their welcome
>   A rid   B remove   C replace   D away
>
> **4** Episodes are written months in advance, so the characters can never talk about the ___ news, sport results, pop records, films, or TV programmes.
>   A ultimate   B latest   C final   D last
>
> **5** . . . and one thing these TV characters hardly ___ do, of course, is sit down and watch television . . .
>   A never   B usually   C likely   D ever

Photocopiable © Oxford University Press

2.13 Avoiding multiple-choice traps

LEVEL   **Lower-intermediate and above**

AIMS   **To practise answering multiple-choice and true/false questions**

TIME   **30 minutes**

PREPARATION   Choose a multiple-choice or true/false reading comprehension exercise with distractors like these:

 i) They contain words which are actually in the text but the overall meaning is different.
 ii) They exaggerate by using *all, always, everybody,* or *never*.
 iii) They say something that may be true but is not stated in the text.

PROCEDURE

1 If learners are experienced at answering multiple-choice or true/false questions, ask them what kind of difficulties they have had answering them in the past.

2 On the board or OHP, write up categories (i), (ii), and (iii) above. Add other techniques the students may have noticed in the question papers they have worked with, such as:

– using words from the text near to where the answer is;
– options which seem plausible but use a different verb tense from that in the text;
– using a word with one meaning in the text and a different meaning in the option;
– options which reflect incorrect interpretation of reference words (see exercise 1.9) in the text.

Give each a number: (iv), (v), and so on.

3 They answer the exam questions in the usual way, and write (i), (ii), or whatever against distractors according to the techniques used. This could be done in groups.

4 Discuss each one as a class.

Example

... But will this language necessarily be English? Some point to the low birth rate in countries where English is strong compared to parts of the world where the population is growing far more quickly. Even in Europe the position of English no longer goes unchallenged. As German economic influence grows, so does the use of a language spoken by nearly 100 million people right in the heart of the continent. English, in contrast, is the first language of only one European state—and that a country widely seen as being unsure whether it belongs in Europe at all ...

The English language is
a the international means of communication in business.
b spoken by nearly 100 million continental Europeans.
c in danger of losing its dominant position.
d spoken in countries with no population growth.

Photocopiable © Oxford University Press

The correct answer is (c). The others are all plausible but have problems: (a) may well be true but is not stated in the text; (b) uses words from the text, but about another language; (d) overstates the case by using *no*.

COMMENTS

This activity can also be used with similar listening comprehension tasks.

2.14 Jumbled multiple-choice

LEVEL   **Intermediate and above**

AIMS   **To practise multiple-choice questions and reading for specific information**

TIME   **30–60 minutes**

PREPARATION   1 Take a reading passage with several multiple-choice questions from past exam papers or practice tests.

2 For each question, highlight the part (or parts) of the text that show which is the correct option. Underline or use one colour—green, for example.

3 Now highlight the parts which relate to the wrong answers (the distractors) by drawing a wavy line underneath or by using a different colour—red, possibly.

4 Put the options in a different order from the relevant information in the text.

Example

> She went to the kitchen and phoned Frau Bauer's mother in Salzburg. Sorry about the outrageous hour but with a death, that's how it goes, she said. Herr Pym is remaining in London for a few days, she said. Why don't you take advantage of Herr Pym's absence and have a nice rest? she said. When she came back it was Lumsden's turn to say his piece. 1) She got his drift immediately and after that she deliberately stopped hearing him. 'Just to fill in any awkward blanks, Mary . . . So that we're all speaking the same language, Mary . . . While Nigel is still closeted with Ambass . . . In case, which God forbid, the odious press gets on to it before it's all cleared up, Mary . . .' (2) Lumsden had a cliché for every occasion and (3) a reputation for being nimble-minded. 'Anyway, that's the route Ambass would like us all to go,' he ended, (4) using the very latest in daring jargon. 'Not unless we're asked, naturally. But if we are. And Mary he sends terrific love. He's with you all the way. And with Magnus too, naturally. Terrific condolences, all that.'

(from *A Perfect Spy* by John le Carré)

Mary did not listen to Lumsden because
a he had a boring way of speaking.
b he was using technical words.
c she did not like what he was saying.
d he was known to be unintelligent.

PROCEDURE	1 Explain to the class what 'distractors' are and how they often correspond to parts of the text.
	2 Working alone, students match each option—(a), (b), (c), (d)—to the relevant part(s) of the text (1, 2, 3, 4).
	3 In pairs, students compare their answers (see key at end of chapter).
	4 The class comment on why each option is right or wrong and how some students might be misled by the distractors.
VARIATION 1	With groups above intermediate level the order of the questions can also be jumbled.
VARIATION 2	Students work out for themselves which is the best option, (a), (b), (c), or (d).
COMMENTS	The example given also shows how task completion is quite possible without understanding every word of a text: perhaps 'drift', 'nimble-minded' and 'daring jargon' in this case.

2.15 Words from the texts

LEVEL	**Lower intermediate and above**
AIMS	**To practise using the dictionary; to build vocabulary**
TIME	**30 minutes +**
PREPARATION	Make sure that all pairs have a monolingual English dictionary.
PROCEDURE	1 The class quickly read a reading comprehension text for gist.
	2 Student A studies the first half of the text and makes a note of the new words it contains and—without letting his or her partner see what the words are—looks them up in the dictionary and makes a list of the definitions, together with the number of the paragraph they are in. Student B does the same with the vocabulary in the second half of the text. You should point out that only words with one meaning should be chosen.
	3 The students exchange lists of definitions. Student A looks at the second part of the text and student B at the first. They match the definitions to the words.

Example

> (paragraph 3)
> He did not think he was telling her a lie when he said he was coming back. Her offer to forward his clothes touched his heart, and at the end of the road he stood and asked himself if he should go back to her. He would miss the train if he waited another minute, and he ran on. And he would have missed the train if he had not met a car. Once he was in the car he felt himself safe—the country was already behind him. The train and the boat at Cork were mere formalities; he was already in America.
> (paragraph 4)
> And when the tall skyscraper rose up beyond the harbour, he felt the thrill of home that he had not found in his native village and wondered how it was that the smell of the bar seemed more natural than the smell of fields, and the roar of crowds more welcome than the silence of the lake's edge.

from 'Untilled Field' by G. Moore (1981: 95)

Definitions (paragraph numbers in brackets):

a noun—statement made by somebody knowing that it is not true (3)
b verb—to send or pass goods or information to somebody (3)
c adj—nothing more than; no better or more important than (3)
d noun—very tall modern city building (4)
e noun—area of water protected from the open sea by land or walls, in which ships can shelter (4)
f noun—wave of physical feeling accompanying strong emotion (4)
g noun—long loud deep sound, especially like that made by a lion (4)

Oxford Advanced Learner's Dictionary (5th edition)

4 Students do the exam task.

VARIATION

With more advanced classes, the definitions can be given in jumbled order.

COMMENTS

Point out to students that whether or not dictionaries are allowed in the actual exam, it is vital that they learn how to use them efficiently as resource books—for working both alone and in class. Do remind them, though, that the first step when they encounter a new word is to try to work out its meaning from the context.

2.16 Finding the clues

LEVEL

Elementary and above

AIM

To guide students to the relevant information in multiple matching, including gapped texts

TIME

45 minutes

PREPARATION

1 Select two multiple matching tasks like the one in the example below.

2 For all but one of the gaps in the first task, highlight a pair of expressions which link the missing paragraph to the main text.

PROCEDURE

1 The students study the first task. Tell them which expressions to highlight on their question papers.

2 The students do the exam task, using these expressions as clues to guide them to the correct answers.

3 Go through the answers, discussing the relevance of the clues.

4 The students do the second exam task. Check their answers (see key at end of chapter).

5 In groups, students discuss the linking expressions which helped them, and highlight them in the text. Monitor each group's progress, pointing out how incorrect links can lead to wrong answers.

6 Groups report back to the class.

Example

You are going to read a magazine article about skywriting. Eight paragraphs have been removed from the article. Choose from the paragraphs A–I the one which fits each gap (14–20). There is one extra paragraph which you do not need to use. There is an example at the beginning (0).

ADMIRING THE SKILLS OF THE AMERICAN SKYWRITERS

Skywriting isn't quite a dying art, but you have to scan the American skies pretty carefully these days to find white smoke puffing out a message. Skywriters have a skill that's seen by nearly all, but no more than a dozen pilots in the USA regularly practise it.

0	I

With <u>this information</u>, gunners on the ground could more easily aim their fire at the enemy beneath the smoke. In the mid-1920s a US company began the first advertising campaign in the sky, promoting cigarettes. The plane flew over Philadelphia sending out a message in the air to the people below. This is how skywriting began and it has continued to fascinate us.

14	

The <u>memory of that moment</u> stayed with him when he followed in his father's footsteps as a pilot and now, as head of the Aerial Sign Company in Hollywood, it comes back when he puts floating adverts up in the sky himself.

15	

<u>He</u> says the pilots need to be highly skilled: 'Most skywriters work about two miles high. Everything has to be square, otherwise it's simply poor penmanship that everybody sees. You have to know where your plane is at all times.'

16	

Together they try it out on the runway, taking half-steps at different corners and turning at angles to be followed in the sky later on.

17	

Pepsi-Cola certainly agrees. Fourteen years ago the soft drink company, searching for someone to carry on a tradition begun in the early 1930s, looked through some 3,000 applicants for a skywriter, and chose a 21-year-old woman pilot from Oregon.

18	

She says that when you are two miles away from your audience, you forget how big an impression it makes on the people below. Kids stop playing ball and traffic comes to a complete standstill. She can't actually see while she's writing, of course. But during the descent and on landing she can look back and see what she's written.

19	

Children come up to Asbury-Oliver after her shows. She says that they are really curious because they are learning to write and form their own letters and they imagine her aeroplane as a pencil. Their parents are often surprised when they meet her.

20	

Each letter is about half a mile across, so a simple IT'S FESTIVAL TIME!, including punctuation and spacing, takes up about eight miles of sky!

A Butler's newest pupil is his 26-year-old son, and Dad shows Junior a diagram he has sketched out to put his wife's name, Regla, up in the air. The drawing looks like her name backwards, as if in a mirror, with arrows, angles, numbers of seconds, and dotted lines showing the pilot what to do.

B Today that same woman, Suzanne Asbury-Oliver, flies twenty or thirty times a year above festivals and fairs. Suzanne and her husband, Steve, who flies aerobatic manoeuvres, live in Colorado but keep their planes in Illinois.

C Jim Butler remembers the day as a kid in the 1950s in New Hampshire when he looked up from his backyard to see a plane writing in the skies.

D 'You'd think it was nothing special to have a woman skywriter, but parents will bring their little girls to meet me. At first they'll approach my husband and say, 'Look what he did,' and he'll say, 'No, she did that.' They're astonished.'

E She gets great pleasure out of doing it well. 'If it's a beautiful day and the letters are staying, you say to yourself, I did a good job. If a letter isn't quite right, you become your own worst critic, and you say, I can't believe I did that.'

F What's more, Butler doesn't get as much business from industry as he used to and isn't sure how much longer he will continue training skywriters.

G 'For me to train a skywriter,' Butler says, in his office in North Perry Airport, 'they have to be able to fly straight and parallel lines and judge their work without using equipment.'

H 'Women are better students in skywriting,' Butler continues, back inside. 'They pay more attention to detail, and they're less likely to depart from procedure.'

I The art began almost eighty years ago in the skies over Europe during the First World War, when a British pilot squirted some light oil into his plane's exhaust system to make a mid-air spot of smoke above an enemy position.

(*Cambridge First Certificate*, Revised 1996)

COMMENTS

The extra paragraph used in multiple matching tasks is designed to reduce the 'jigsaw effect' of the last answer falling into place by elimination. Giving no clues for one matching pair of paragraphs avoids re-creating this effect.

FOLLOW-UP

In future multiple matching tasks, students highlight the expressions which led them to their answers. This should make it easier for you to show them where they are going wrong if they find this task type difficult.

VARIATION 1

With lower level classes, give more than one clue per gap, adding—for example—*the enemy/War* to gap 0, *his father's/as a kid* to 14 and *the pilots/they have to be able to fly* to 15.

VARIATION 2

This technique can also be used with multiple matching tasks that require students to read for specific information. Highlight key expressions in the extracts and proceed as above:

You are going to read some information about holiday companies. For question 21–35, choose from the extracts (A–E). Some of the companies may be chosen more than once. When more than one answer is required, these may be given in any order. There is an example at the beginning (0).

Which company or companies:
includes some free food in their holidays?

0	B

COMPANY B
Our city selection offers inclusive short break holidays to over 30 cities. You can travel on a flight of your choice and select your accommodation from one star to luxury hotels. We grade our hotels according to standard of comfort and position. Our flexibility also enables us to deal speedily with late bookings right up to the date of departure and we never charge a late booking fee.

In your travel pack you will find: tickets, specially marked maps, restaurant vouchers, etc. For most of our cities we enclose a booklet entitled 'how to spend less and have more fun . . .', which gives you excellent and much appreciated advice.

(*Cambridge First Certificate*, Revised 1996)

Answers

2.1 1 as/while/when   2 my   3 was   4 proved   5 with   6 I
7 must   8 else   9 had   10 way
2.3 1E 2H 3B 4F 5A 6G 7D
2.6 D and A
2.13 c
2.16 14C   15G   16A   17H   18B   19E   20D

3 Writing

The activities in this chapter will help prepare students for examination papers such as 'Writing', 'Composition', 'Written English', 'Commentary and Essay', and 'Test of Written English'.

Candidates in most examinations are expected to be able to give information and opinions, report events, and write descriptions. The language used should be appropriate to the purpose and intended reader. At lower levels this may entail writing, for example, notes, messages, postcards, instructions, short narratives, or personal letters, while more advanced students may have to write reports, applications, articles, advertisements, business letters, summaries, or various kinds of essay. Some tasks involve a response to stimuli such as a reading text or a series of prompts. Success usually requires completing the tasks set with accurate grammar, spelling, and punctuation; adequate vocabulary; suitable layout and clear handwriting; cohesion within the text; and a style appropriate to the context. In exams such as Cambridge CCSE or the Oxford-Arels exams, however, the main consideration is communicative competence.

Whichever exam students take, though, a vital first consideration is careful reading of the instructions—in many cases it is impossible to achieve the pass mark if the task is not completed, no matter how good the language used may be. Instructions are the main focus of 3.9 (see also 1.5), while the related exam skill of planning written work is dealt with in 3.1, as is timing: spending the right amount of time on each stage of the writing is essential for successful task completion (see also 1.10). Activity 3.1 includes another vital exam skill: checking written work, which also features in 1.11.

Particular attention is paid to different types of essay question: narrative (3.5, 3.6, 3.7), as in Cambridge PET, FCE, CAE, and CPE, IELTS, and Trinity; discursive (3.4, 3.8), as in FCE and CPE, MELAB, the IB, the TOEFL Test in Written English, and the IOL Diploma; and descriptive (3.3), as in FCE and CPE, MELAB, and Pitman. Other kinds of writing task covered include formal and informal letter writing (3.10, 3.11, 3.12), as used in PET, FCE, CAE and CPE, the Oxford-Arels exams, Trinity, and the ICC; writing summaries or résumés (3.14, 3.15), as in CPE, the Oxford-Arels Higher, and the IOL Diploma and Intermediate Diploma; writing about set or prescribed books (3.15), as in CPE and FCE, the IB, and the IOL Diploma; and expanding notes to form complete texts (3.13, see also 4.7), as in CAE and the Oxford-Arels Higher.

Many of the activities aimed at one task type can be used for others—for example, many of the skills developed by narrative essay writing can be transferred to report writing.

Preparation for most exams inevitably means the teacher has to correct a lot of written work, but students can take on some of the load by checking each other's writing (3.4, 3.5, 3.11, see also 4.5), which gives useful practice at identifying and correcting errors, as well as raising awareness of the kinds of mistakes that interfere with communication—for example, when students have to ask the writer of the text what is really meant. Self-correction is encouraged in 3.1 (see also 1.11) and the correction code in the Introduction (page 8) or the modified code in 4.4 can be used, on the basis that the best approach to error is to make students work it out for themselves. Right from the start of the course, students should get into the habit of keeping all their extended writing work for future reference.

As many exam writing tasks require effective reading on the part of the candidate (which of course reflects a common pattern in the outside world), a number of activities also help build reading skills, for example reading for gist (3.9), main points (3.5), and specific language (3.8). Reading texts are used as models for writing in 3.5 and 3.8.

Getting started is often a problem for students when faced with exam instructions, so 3.3 focuses on writing introductory paragraphs. Awareness of the language functions that need to be expressed—persuading, apologizing, or instructing, for example—is essential for successful task completion: this is practised in 3.10. Help is given with linking and sequencing text in 3.7 and 3.8.

Appropriacy of language use is another important factor in proficient writing both in the exam room and in the wider world. The kind of language needed for writing a company report is clearly quite different from that used in a message for a child, and if the two are mixed up the writer's aim is unlikely to be achieved. Special emphasis, therefore, is placed on appropriacy in 3.12 (see also 3.2, 3.9), and throughout this chapter students are encouraged to think about the reason why they are writing.

3.1 Essay planning and timing

LEVEL	Elementary and above
AIMS	To focus on planning, timing, and checking written work
TIME	60 minutes +

PREPARATION

Ensure a plentiful supply of writing paper similar in size and line spacing to that used in the actual exam.

PROCEDURE

1 Set a writing task but tell the class that for the moment they are to write the essay plan only. Suggest they first note down ideas, then group them according to paragraphs, and, finally, write down any words or phrases that might be useful. Set a time limit of about ten minutes.

2 Check their work and make suggestions when necessary.

3 Students write the essay on the paper provided. Set the same time limit as in the exam, but deduct the time used for planning and a similar amount of time for checking at the end.

4 Students check their work for (among other things) correct:
– vocabulary
– tense formation and usage
– word order
– register (formal/informal words, contractions, etc.)
– use and non-use of articles
– punctuation/capitalization
– spelling
– linking (between clauses, sentences, and paragraphs)
– agreement (subject/verb, demonstrative/noun, etc.)

5 Students count up the number of words and the number of lines they have used, and work out the average words per line. To save time in future essays they count the number of lines only. Calculating and using the number used in blocks of 3 or 5 lines is an even more efficient way of staying within the word limit.

6 Get everybody to draw a table something like the one below, and then complete it.

Example

Fill in the time you should spend on each stage of your writing.	
Stage	*Minutes*
1 Choose essay subject	....
2 Ideas	....
3 Organization	....
4 Useful language	....
5 Introductory paragraph	....
6 1st main paragraph	....
7 2nd main paragraph	....
8 Concluding paragraph	....
9 Checking	....

7 Check the answers. Suggest changes in the number of minutes where necessary.

FOLLOW-UP

When setting an essay for homework, get all the students to plan it in class—perhaps just before the end of the lesson—and have a look at what they have written. Perhaps give a mark for the quality of the plan.

COMMENTS

1 Stress the need for effective planning, timing, and checking of written work, pointing out that examiners will be looking for good organization and a high degree of accuracy in their essays. It is also essential for students to get used to working with a time limit well before they actually do the exam.

2 To reinforce the points made, it may be advisable to do this activity more than once.

3.2 Essay marks

LEVEL

Intermediate and above

AIMS

To focus on essay marking; to practise essay writing, intensive reading, and error correction; to encourage discussion of written work

TIME

30 minutes + 15 minutes in next lesson

PREPARATION

Obtain sample essays with examiners' marks and comments, if available. Otherwise write your own assessments on work by students from another class or a previous course (but do ask their permission). Make two sets of class copies, one of them without the marking.

PROCEDURE

1 Elicit comments on one of the unmarked essays and ask the class to suggest a mark. Then put the examiners' comments and mark on the board or OHP.

2 Students in pairs study another unmarked sample essay, write their comments at the bottom, and estimate the mark.

3 Give the students copies of the same essay with the examiners' comments and mark. They compare these with their own copies.

Example

Dear Madam,

I'm writing to you to apply for the post of firefighter advertised in the news on the beginning of last month.

This work is perfect for me because I have worked during three years in a fire brigade for the protection of the wild forests in Greece.

I like the danger and I'm a person who likes taking the risks.

So, I would be pleased if you choose me for this post. If you want to contact with me, write to me or call me in the 7771458. I'm looking forward to hearing from you.

Yours sincerely

Examiner's comments
This is a brief but effective realization of the task, despite the rather informal style. The candidate has some difficulties with prepositions and articles, but her vocabulary is adequate, the letter is largely free of spelling and punctuation errors, and her use of tenses is good. Band: 3.

Photocopiable © Oxford University Press

4 Set an essay, perhaps for homework.

5 In pairs students correct and give a mark for each other's work.

6 Students discuss the essay and the marking.

7 Check the essays and the marking.

VARIATION

1 Obtain a copy of the examining board's essay-marking criteria. Bear in mind that for some exams these change quite often.

2 Break down all the descriptors to sentence or phrase level and jumble them up. Put the marking bands in a column alongside.

3 Using their monolingual English dictionaries where necessary, groups of students match the parts of the descriptors with the marking bands.

Match two of the descriptors on the right with each of the marking bands on the left. 5 is the best, 0 is the worst.

5	Sufficiently natural, errors only when more complex language attempted.
4	Totally inadequate attempt at task.
	Serious lack of control and/or frequent basic errors.
3	Good attempt at task, only minor omissions.
	Some evidence of range of vocabulary and structure.
2	Register acceptable though reader would need to make allowances.
	Totally positive effect on target reader.
1	Errors sometimes obscure communication and/or language too elementary.
0	Use of English satisfactory though lacking variety and range.
	No sufficient comprehensible language for assessment.
	Minimal errors: resourceful, controlled and natural use of language.
	Occasional serious errors should not impede communication.

3.3 Opening paragraphs

LEVEL

Lower-intermediate and above

AIMS

To practise evaluating and writing introductory paragraphs; to practise writing descriptions

TIME

30 minutes

PREPARATION

1 Choose a descriptive essay title that has already been done by another class. You will need 4–6 answer scripts.

2 Cut and paste the opening paragraph from each script, making a short photocopiable worksheet. Put the title at the top.

3 Prepare six more essay titles that set the same kind of task.

PROCEDURE

1 Hand out the worksheets. Each student corrects any errors.

2 Go through the errors with the class.

3 Elicit the characteristics of a good opening paragraph, such as giving background information; making a generalization which has to be justified; arousing the reader's interest in a person or an event; why the writer is interested in the subject; why the topic is controversial.

4 In groups, students discuss which paragraphs use which techniques and report back to the class.

5 Still in groups, students write their own opening paragraph for the same title.

7 Working individually, students practise writing opening paragraphs for the other titles.

Example

(These are uncorrected extracts from students' work.)

Describe the laziest person you know.

a Being lazy is one of the worst features of modern society. The world we live in today, requires active and responsable people who do not have this sickness, called lazyness.

b It is difficult to decide who is the laziest person I know, but after a brief thought I think I know who this person can be. It is a girl who goes with me to school, her name is Isabel.

c My Uncle Charles is the laziest person I've ever known. He's tall, thin. He wears small glasses, he's got dark brown hair turning grey. He's 45 or at least that's what he says but I really doubt about it. He's single and that's not strange: he's been too lazy to look for a girlfriend.

d Nigel is a friend of mine and I believe that he is the laziest person I know. He is so lazy that he doesn't do anything by himself. He waits for the others to do the things for him. And when I say the others I mean basicly his mother.

Other possible essay titles:

– Write about your best friend.
– It is your first day at a new school. Write a description of your teacher.
– Describe one of the main characters in the book you have read.
– An English-language news magazine is preparing a supplement about your country. Write an **article** for this magazine about someone who is nationally famous.
– Think of two films which feature the same actor. Contrast the personalities of the two different characters which this person plays.

FOLLOW-UP   1 Using the opening paragraph they like best, students write their own text based on the same title.

2 When they have finished, give each student a copy of the text by the original writer of the opening paragraph and let them compare.

COMMENTS

Do remember to get students' permission to use their scripts, as some may be unhappy at having their work read by others.

3.4 For and against

LEVEL

Intermediate and above

AIMS

To improve discursive writing skills

TIME

45 minutes

PREPARATION

Find an example of a balanced discursive essay and make copies for the class. Make sure every student has pens or markers in two different colours. Alternatively use straight and wavy underlining, as in the example below.

PROCEDURE

1 Students go through the text, highlighting all the arguments *for* in one colour (or with straight underlining) and all the arguments *against* in another (or with wavy underlining).

2 Ask the class if they can spot—and correct—any of the language mistakes. Then elicit the positive aspects: the introduction, the balanced number of points on either side in two main paragraphs, the short conclusion giving the writer's point of view, and the discourse markers (see 3.8) she uses: *Another point is . . ., On the other hand . . ., Personally . . .*, etc.

3 Write an essay title on the board: *Military service should be abolished. Discuss* or *All cities should be car-free. Discuss*, for example. In groups, students brainstorm arguments on both sides and report back to the class. Write notes on the board under 'for' and 'against' headings.

4 Groups write an opening paragraph (see 3.3) and compare with other groups.

5 Set the essay task for homework. Tell students to leave about ten lines blank after each main paragraph.

6 In the next lesson students exchange their completed essays with their partners, who highlight the points on either side to show how far balance has been achieved. Encourage them to suggest more ideas to each other, which they can write in the spaces they have left.

7 Collect in their work and check.

Example

'The ideal lifestyle would consist of sport and leisure'. Discuss.

Sport can be understood as a way to keep your body fit, or as competition, and leisure can be just doing nothing or doing what you like best. In a lifestyle of sport and leisure the four meanings would be included and the problems and advantages without one of them would change slightly.

Beginning with the problems, the first one would be the integration in society of <u>disabled people</u>. Although leisure could help to mitigate it, living in a society in which sport is so important could mean frustration because most of sport is just competition. Also, as people would be much more interested in their body than in their brain, <u>intellectual development</u> which is absolutely necessary for human evolution, would stop or go very slowly. Another point is that some people need to be compelled to do things. With this lifestyle they would not do anything and they would fall in a complete <u>apathy</u> towards life.

On the other hand there are all the advantages this lifestyle would entail. Leisure and sport would not be seen as losing our time so a more relaxed society would appear. People would also be <u>healthier</u> because sport could fight many illnesses caused by stress and a sedentary life. Leisure would consist in doing what you want when you want and this involves studying too. More people would be interested because they do it by their own.

Personally I do not think an ideal lifestyle exists because it depends on everyone's capacities and tastes. My ideal lifestyle would be a balance between sport, leisure, and work.

3.5 Model texts

LEVEL	**Lower-intermediate and above**
AIMS	**To practise using a comprehension text as a narrative writing model**
TIME	**60 minutes**
PREPARATION	1 Choose a narrative reading comprehension text from past papers or practice tests. Passages from biographical and historical sources are particularly useful, as are extracts from novels and sports reports. The text should contain some of the following:

– past forms of *there is/there are*;
– reference words such as *this* and *that*;
– conjunctions of time like *after, while, then, until*, or *as soon as*;
– reported speech;

– tense sequences using (for example) the past simple, continuous, or perfect;

– *-ing* forms such as *Before doing* . . . and *Having done* . . .;

2 Make a list of the main events from the story in jumbled order.

3 Prepare two or three narrative essay titles.

PROCEDURE

1 Point out features of narrative texts, such as setting the scene (saying who, what, where, and when), moving to another scene, hints about later events, sudden setbacks and surprises, varying sentence length to change the pace, creating suspense, a well-planned ending.

2 The class does the reading comprehension exam task. Check the answers.

3 Working individually, students put the events from the (by now familiar) text in the correct order (see key at end of chapter).

4 They compare answers with their partners. Check and ask the class which of the grammatical forms mentioned in Preparation 1 are used and what difficulties they had, such as the use of the past perfect to indicate a previous event.

5 In pairs, students scan the text for some of the features mentioned in Procedure 1. Get students to highlight or note down the words or sentences which illustrate them. Then go through them as a class.

6 Give a choice of narrative essay titles for homework. Encourage the use of grammar and narrative writing techniques from the reading text.

7 Before they hand it in, pairs check each other's work for mistakes and identify as many of the features from stage 1 as they can.

8 If the students who wrote them don't mind, put some of the best stories on the classroom wall for others to read.

Example

Liverpool had eventually overcome Everton in the FA Cup and now faced a League game against the side they would meet in the Final, Manchester United. In the event it was an easy victory against a team that made little effort to compete, their thoughts clearly elsewhere. This extended Liverpool's lead to four points, and after drawing with QPR they were left needing just a single point to clinch the title.

With the FA and European Cup Finals still to come, a goalless match at Coventry secured yet another Championship for the Reds and the bookies' odds against a unique treble shortened even further.

But disappointment was to follow. Manchester United somehow managed to win the FA Cup Final, leaving Liverpool just a few days to bounce back in time for the match against Borussia Moenchengladbach.

Few outside Merseyside gave them much chance of winning their first ever European Champions Cup. But on a night in Rome of incredible emotion, Tommy Smith's goal set up a 3–1 victory and celebrations which lasted until dawn.

How many of the six matches did Liverpool win?
a Two. **b** Three. **c** Four. **d** Five.

Put the matches in the order they were played:

a v Coventry (League)

b v Manchester United (FA Cup)

c v QPR (League)

d v Borussia Moenchengladbach (European Cup)

e v Everton (FA Cup)

f v Manchester United (League)

Write the story of one of the following:

– a successful sports person or team from your country;

– someone who succeeded despite a severe disability;

– a person who risked his or her life to save others.

3.6 Telling the story

LEVEL

Lower-intermediate and above

AIMS

To improve narrative writing skills; to encourage intensive reading and listening; to practise oral storytelling and discussion

TIME

20 minutes + 20 minutes in next lesson

PREPARATION

Set a narrative essay for homework, preferably from a choice of topics. Ask the students to make a special effort with the ending, which should refer back to the theme of the story.

Example

Write a story entitled 'A Lucky Escape'.

. . . 'Suddenly it all became clear: they had been watching my every move and only that last-minute change of plan had saved me from disaster.'

PROCEDURE

1 In the next lesson, get the students to write down the last sentence from their essay on a piece of paper.

2 The students work in pairs. They show the last sentences to their partners, who try to guess the plot of the essay.

3 Collect in the pieces of paper and assign numbers to the most interesting endings, for example those which give some idea of the plot in relatively few words and the ones that end in suspense, with a moral to the story, or with a clear conclusion. Avoid surprise endings.

4 Read out some of the endings. Students must choose one (other than their partner's) as the last sentence of their next essay task. They should make a note of the number they choose.

5 Ask which numbers have been chosen and then dictate the sentences so that students can copy them down.

6 Students write up their essays for homework.

7 In the next lesson those who have chosen the same numbers form groups and compare their essays.

8 The class find out who wrote the sentence they used by asking around. They form new groups and compare with the original essays. Then you collect them all in to correct.

> **Some final sentences from students' narrative essays**
>
> 1 Coincidence? Luck? Destiny? I don't know, so next time instead of taking the bus try taking the underground: you never know how the day might end up!
>
> 2 He treated the people around him badly and now the world has done the same with him.
>
> 3 I couldn't wait to see that town behind me: home was just several hours ahead.
>
> 4 I wish my parents hadn't gone on holidays and what's more they hadn't come back so quickly.
>
> 5 I even wrote a letter to her telling how much I loved her and asking her for a date, but I wasn't brave enough to post it and I tore it into pieces.

Photocopiable © Oxford University Press

COMMENTS Point out to the class the importance of writing good endings, perhaps by showing them some examples from novels, short stories, magazine stories, writing skills books, and readers.

3.7 Continuing the story

LEVEL **Lower-intermediate and above**

AIMS **To practise using discourse markers in narrative essays**

TIME **30–60 minutes**

PREPARATION 1 Write a maximum of eight different narrative essay introductions on separate pieces of paper or on the OHP.

2 Put a list of discourse markers on the board, for example: *next, so, because of this, on the other hand, however, instead, actually, incidentally, at the same time, in the end.* If necessary, explain their meanings and use.

PROCEDURE 1 If there are more than eight students in the class, put them into groups.

2 Give each student in the class or group a different opening sentence and tell them to add a few sentences or a short paragraph. What they write must be linked to what has gone before, so encourage them to use the expressions you have written on the board.

3 After about five minutes—more if the class or group is small—students stop writing and pass their stories on to the student sitting on their right.

4 Students read what has already been written and then add to it, writing for the same amount of time as before.

5 This continues until everyone in the class or group has contributed to all the essays and/or a complete story has been written.

6 Each student reads out the story in their possession to the rest of the class or group. Others can correct errors when they have finished, bearing in mind that students tend to be less sensitive about being corrected when the mistakes are not theirs!

7 If they have been working in groups, get each group to choose a story to read out to the rest of the class.

Possible narrative essay beginnings

– Now I was completely on my own. Not knowing what to expect, I walked out of the station and into the middle of that huge city . . .

– The whole country had known for ages that it was wrong and at last I was in a position to do something about it . . .

– I was woken up by someone shouting 'Fire!'. There was smoke coming under the door so I jumped out of bed and . . .

– The exam had begun. I picked up the question papers, looked through them and . . .

– When the sun came up I saw that I was on a desert island. Then I realized I was not quite alone . . .

– Of course I didn't believe in ghosts, but there was certainly something strange about that old house . . .

VARIATION

This activity can take place while students are working on other tasks which require lengthy individual study. A single story moving around the class can provide a welcome break, for instance, from reading comprehension or written grammar exercises. When the story has been read out, ask the class if they can think of a title for it.

3.8 Building an argument

LEVEL	**Upper-intermediate and above**
AIMS	**To focus on discourse markers; to develop discursive writing skills**
TIME	**45 minutes**
PREPARATION	**1** From the opinion pages of newspapers or magazines, choose at least two articles which deal with subjects that are of general topical interest. **2** Select one and remove the linking expressions such as *besides*, *on the other hand*, or *therefore*, as well as argument-building phrases like *It is obvious that* or *It seems to me*. Make a list of them in jumbled order.
PROCEDURE	**1** Explain the function of discourse markers in building an argument, for example the use of 'On the one hand . . .' to signal that the writer is going to make a contrast, or 'Finally . . .' to indicate his or her intention to conclude. **2** Go through the meanings of the expressions in the list. **3** Students replace the missing words and phrases in the gaps.

Example

Fill in the blanks with these expressions:

even if	There is no doubt that	While this may
likely to be	What is not so clear is	
In a society where	If . . . is anything to go by	
simply because	not just . . . but	To some extent

___ (1) virtually all transactions are done in plastic, to be poorly rated has become a matter ___ of inconvenience ___ (2) of genuine social stigma. Americans are finding that credit ratings both open and close doors.

___ (3) Britain is following America towards a cashless society. The move away from cash has been accelerated by the introduction of debit cards such as Switch and Delta, which now outnumber credit cards.

'___ (4), credit card usage is growing ___ (5) people have become conditioned to pay with something plastic,' says the Credit Card Research Group.

___ (6) spell disaster to many, the combination of more astute cardholders and conservative lending is likely to prevent the excesses of the 1980s recurring, ___ (7) the elusive 'feelgood' factor emerges.

___ (8), the role cards and access to credit will have in shaping society.

___ the American example ___ (9), the victims of the next stage in the credit boom are ___ (10) the careless.

The Sunday Times

4 Check the answers and write some or all of them on the board in roughly the same position they were used in the text, for example:

In a society where ....
.... not just .... but ....

A key appears at the end of the chapter.

5 Ask the class to suggest a different topic and elicit a new text using the same discourse markers:

In a society where *more and more people are going to university, having good qualifications is* not just *an advantage* but *a necessity.*

6 Hand out the rest of the articles. In pairs, students underline all the similar expressions they can find. They discuss their meaning and usage.

7 Using some of these expressions, students write an essay (for homework) on one of the article topics as it relates to their world. For example:

Do you think credit cards will one day replace cash in your country?

6 Before handing their work in, students in pairs assess each other's essay for content, form, grammar, and vocabulary, paying particular attention to the use of discourse markers.

3.9 Essay instructions

LEVEL	**Lower-intermediate and above**
AIMS	**To practise studying and following instructions for written work**
TIME	**60 minutes**
PREPARATION	**1** Make photocopies of an essay, article, report, account, or letter written by a student from another class on a topic that has not been done by your present class. Delete any instructions, titles, letter headings, salutations, etc.
	2 Write four plausible instructions or titles to add to the original as a multiple-choice task.
PROCEDURE	**1** Hand out the text, pointing out that clues to its source have been removed. Students study it and decide which is the original instruction or title. They explain why the other three are unlikely.

2 Students choose one of the other three titles and do the task. When they have finished they give their work to their partner, who compares it with the photocopied text. Ask the class what differences they have noticed between the two, particularly in terms of organization, content, and register.

Example (extract)

Nobody and nothing is perfect. So is life—full of problems. This town faces a lot of problems that make the way of life more difficult.

First the government must set better time tables in the bus stops. In fact there aren't any time tables at all, at least where I live, and people don't know what time do the buses pass. This is a very big problem because people, who don't have cars or motorbikes, are usually late at work and the children, who live far away from school and take the local bus, are usually late too.

Which of the following—a, b, c, or d—is the most likely instruction for the above text?

a Write an article for a tourist brochure about bus services in your town.

b You have just moved to a new town. Write a letter to your best friend saying what it is like.

c Write an article for your college magazine suggesting ways of improving life in your town.

d You work in a local government office. Write a report for the council about the public transport system.

Photocopiable © Oxford University Press

FOLLOW-UP 1

Repeat Preparation with a script that does *not* follow the instructions given, or use a published sample essay which answers a slightly different question. Include among the four options both the exam question and the question which the essay answers. Students study the texts and consider the differences they reflect, then discuss as a class.

FOLLOW-UP 2

The class are shown a text and asked to write the instructions themselves.

VARIATION

With lower-level classes, do just stages 1 and 2.

COMMENTS

Point out to the class that working carefully through instructions in this way will help them avoid the common mistake of writing essays that are not relevant to the instructions.

3.10 Writing informal letters

LEVEL	**Intermediate and above**
AIMS	**To identify language functions and practise letter writing**
TIME	**60 minutes**
PREPARATION	1 Choose a model letter from the coursebook or writing skills book and make a note of all the formulaic expressions such as *I'm writing to . . .*, *It was good to . . .*, and *I'd be delighted to . . . .*
	2 Draw up a worksheet with a list of the functions expressed by these formulaic expressions, with space on the right for students to write in the actual words used.
PROCEDURE	1 Check that everyone understands the words used to describe functions.
	2 Working individually, students read the text of the letter and fill in the spaces. Usually the stem of the expression is enough.

Example

Read the letter and note down the words the writer uses to express these ideas. The first one has been done as an example.
(extract)

Dear Alex,

<u>Sorry I haven't</u> been in touch for a while but I've been away for the last couple of weeks, at Tony's place in the mountains in fact.

   Anyway, <u>I was so pleased to hear that you</u>'d passed your exam . . .

1	Apologizing	<u>Sorry I haven't</u>
2	Congratulating	<u>I was so pleased to hear that you</u>
3	Expressing surprise	<u>I'd never have guessed that</u>
4	Accepting	<u>I'd love to</u>
5	Expressing happiness	<u>I'm delighted to hear that</u>
6	Inquiring	<u>do you happen to know if</u>
7	Expressing amusement	<u>so funny that</u>
8	Expressing certainty	<u>there's bound to be</u>
9	Inviting	<u>would you like to</u>
10	Encouraging	<u>good luck with</u>

3 Check for complete accuracy.

4 Students write to their partners using as many of the functions as they can. Assign roles and provide background information. Tell them to write only on the right-hand half of the paper.

5 Students exchange letters and underline or highlight the formulae; to the left of the letter text they write the functions expressed.

6 Students compare with their partners.

Example

> *Read your partner's letter. Write the functions on the left and underline the words which express them in the letter.*
>
> Dear Ana
>
> *apologizing* I'm sorry I couldn't write back sooner but as you know we've been away and I only got back . . .

VARIATION 1

To make it easier for students to find the words in the text, the list of functions can be split up by paragraphs.

VARIATION 2

Follow the same procedure with formal letter writing.

3.11 Who gets the job?

LEVEL

Intermediate and above

AIMS

To practise writing job applications and replying to formal letters

TIME

60 minutes

PREPARATION

1 Ensure students are familiar with the conventions of formal letters in English. For reply writing, practise formulae such as *I am writing in reply to your letter of . . ., I am pleased to be able to . . ., I am afraid that . . ., I would like to point out that . . ., I would be most grateful if you would . . ., I look forward to hearing from you . . ..*

2 From the classified ads section of an English-language newspaper or magazine, choose two jobs that you think your students might be interested in applying for.

3 Write the job descriptions on the board, labelling them A and B. Include a corporate name and brief address, indicating who the letter should be sent to.

PROCEDURE

1 Elicit the qualifications and kind of experience needed for both jobs, noting the suggestions on the board under A and B.

2 All students write applications for both jobs on separate pieces of paper, inventing qualifications and experience where necessary.

3 Divide the class up into equal numbers of Student As and Student Bs.

4 Give each Student A two applications for Job A and each Student B two for Job B.

5 Students read both letters for gist and decide who gets the job.

6 Students correct language errors in both letters.

7 Students write brief replies to both applicants, giving reasons why they have or have not been selected. Suggest formulae such as *We are pleased be able to inform you that . . ., I am afraid that in view of the fact that . . ., We would like to offer you . . ., Although you are clearly an applicant . . . .*

8 Students give their replies to the applicants, along with their corrected letters.

FOLLOW-UP

If this activity goes particularly well—and bearing in mind norms in the students' culture—the applicants who have been rejected (half the class) can write back to protest at the decision by the bosses, who in turn can reply to them. This could be done as homework.

VARIATION

With lower levels, put the class into two halves. One half writes an application for job A and the other applies for job B. In pairs students then read two applications and decide who gets the job. They correct the letters. Finally they write to each applicant explaining briefly why they have or have not been selected.

3.12 Appropriacy

LEVEL

Intermediate and above

AIMS

To help students recognize inappropriate register; to practise writing formal and informal letters

TIME

60 minutes

PREPARATION

1 From past papers, choose two questions which entail writing for very different readers.

2 On a handout or OHP transparency, write double-spaced opening paragraphs for both tasks in completely the wrong register, entertainingly so if possible (exaggerated British reserve is often a favourite with students).

PROCEDURE

1 Go through your texts phrase by phrase, getting students to spot the inappropriate expressions and suggest alternatives to write in between the lines.

2 The class are divided into pairs. Student A is given an exam question requiring formal language (for example, writing a report for the boss), while Student B's question specifies informal language (for example, instructions to a friend looking after the house while you are away)—but they both have to include inappropriate expressions in their writing. Remind them to double space their work.

3 When students have finished, they scan each other's work for register mistakes and write in more appropriate expressions underneath.

Examples

1 *Write a letter of application for an office job in a large company.*

> Hi!
> I really like the look of that job in the ad so I'm writing to ask you a few things about it. How much are you paying? If it's more than I'm getting right now then that would be cool, but it's not just the money I'm after. What about hours and all that stuff? Perhaps I'd better call round for a chat about everything. What sort of time would suit you? I'm kind of busy in the mornings so let's say any time after one. Is that OK or . . .

2 *Write a letter to a boy or girl you would like to go out with.*

> Dear Madam,
> I am taking the liberty of contacting you by letter, notwithstanding the fact that I have yet formally to make your acquaintance. I trust you will forgive me this impertinence as I wish to communicate to you, my good lady, my most sincere sentiments of an amorous and even irrational nature. I earnestly hope that we can arrange a mutually convenient appointment for the not too distant future and that . . .

FOLLOW-UP

Later in the course repeat stages 1–3, but this time using less extreme examples to reflect the kind of appropriacy errors more advanced students are liable to make. More marginal areas could include the choice between the active and the passive, phrasal verbs or verbs of Latin origin, and short or long words in general.

3.13 Expanding notes

LEVEL

Elementary and above

AIMS

To practise note expansion by unscrambling the answers

TIME

30 minutes

PREPARATION

Prepare a number of note-expansion exercises plus answers.

PROCEDURE

1 On the board or OHP, write the instructions and example set of notes from an exercise, leaving plenty of space below.

Example

> Write only one sentence for each set of notes. You may add words and change the form of the words given in the notes but do not add any extra information.
>
> **Position and population:** Pacific state, USA; pop. 23.5m (largest, USA)

(Cambridge Certificate in Advanced English)

2 Underneath, write the words of the answer in jumbled order:
USA largest of is in state 23.5 which Pacific a USA the population with the a is California the of million

3 Elicit each word in the most likely order, punctuating where necessary:
California is a Pacific state of the USA, with a population of 23.5 million, which is the largest in the USA.

4 Put the class into pairs. Give student A a complete expansion exercise together with the answers; hand out a different expansion exercise plus answers to student B.

5 On separate answer sheets, students rewrite each answer in jumbled order.

6 The students exchange exercises (but not the answers) and unscramble the sentences.

7 Students exchange answers, compare them with their sentences, and discuss.

VARIATION

Instead of jumbling the sentences, student A studies the answers and rewrites the sets of notes with the missing parts of speech in brackets between the words (dictionaries may be needed). Student B uses these as clues to write the correct answers.

Example

> **Piraeus**: city, pop. approx. 200,000, port Athens, major ind. and comm. centre.

Student A writes: [article] city [preposition] Piraeus, [preposition] [article] pop. [preposition] approx. 200,000, [verb] [article] port [preposition] Athens [conjunction] [article] major ind. and comm. centre.

Student B writes: The city of Piraeus, with a population of approximately 200,000, is the port of Athens and a major industrial and commercial centre.

COMMENTS   For further practice with this kind of task, see *Learner-based Teaching* by Colin Campbell and Hanna Kryszewska in this series.

3.14 Whose summary?

LEVEL   **Lower-intermediate and above**

AIMS   **To focus on the form, style, and content of summaries; to practise essay and summary writing; to provide extensive reading practice**

TIME   **30–60 minutes**

PREPARATION   None

PROCEDURE   1 Remind the class of what summary writing entails and what the examiners will be looking for, i.e. a concise and well-written paragraph which includes all the relevant points in, where possible, the candidate's own words.

2 Set an extended writing task for homework. It could be a narrative, descriptive or discursive essay, or might involve writing a report, giving instructions, or providing information in some other way, but the important thing is that the content varies from student to student. This should be the case if they write about their own personal experiences, observations, and feelings. For example:

Tell the story of an event which changed your life.
Describe a place which is important to you, or
Give your opinion on an issue which you feel is ignored by other people.

3 In the next lesson, correct students' work as discreetly as possible and hand out the scripts in random order, ensuring that nobody has their own essay.

4 Students summarize all or part of the text they are given in the same way they would for the exam.

5 Students keep the essay but put their name on their summary and pass it to the student on their right.

6 Students read the summary they receive. If it summarizes the essay they wrote they keep it; if not they pass it on again.

7 When all students have the summary of their own text, they pair off with the student who wrote the summary and compare it with the essay. Then they form a pair with the student whose essay they summarized and do the same.

3.15 Writing about books

LEVEL	**Intermediate and above**
AIMS	**To encourage extensive reading and discussion of texts; to practise writing summaries and essays about prescribed books**
TIME	**20 minutes per week**
PREPARATION	None
PROCEDURE	1 Assign one of the set books to half of the class (Student As) and a different set book to the other half (Student Bs). If possible the books should be of approximately similar length. For the first week's homework students do not start reading their book; instead Student A finds out what he or she can about it and writes a summary for Student B. B does the same for A. Encourage them to look at notes on the author, when and where the book was written, and other details from the introduction and blurb. If there is not much information in the book itself, suggest they look for it in encyclopaedias or other reference works.

2 In the next lesson A gives his or her summary to partner B, who asks for further information using *Who/What/Where/When/Which/How/Why?* questions and notes down the answers.

3 For the next week's homework, A reads the first chapter and outlines where and when the story is set, describes the main characters, and indicates the relationship between them.

4 Stage 2 is repeated, but A works with a different B.

5 For homework A summarizes the main events in the next chapter, mentioning his or her own reactions to the people, the plot, the atmosphere, and the way the book is written. This, with a different student B (who asks questions as in stage 2), is repeated for each chapter. Remind everyone to keep the summaries and notes.

6 When A has finished the book, B asks more questions, for example:

- Are the characters convincing?
- Can you identify with any of them?
- Are there scenes that you can picture?
- Is it a good story?
- Does the writer create suspense?
- Are the geographical, historical, and technical details correct?
- Is the ending exciting?
- Is there a moral to the story?

7 A and B write essays (remind them to use mainly the present simple) about their own books using essay titles such as those below, under 'Examples'. For more ideas, form groups of Student As and Bs and get them to write down all the titles relating to their book that they can think of and report back to the class.

8 Shortly before the exam students re-read their own book and, if they found it interesting, read their partners' book too— comparing it with the summaries and their notes as they go along. Not everyone will want to do this, but point out that it should enable them to choose from two set-book essay titles in the exam.

Examples

a How appropriate is the title?
b Describe a significant event in the story and its consequences.
c To what extent is the story probably autobiographical?
d Describe the character you like most or least.
e What does it tell you about society then or now?
f Tell the story from another character's point of view.
g Why do you think the book is so popular?
h Outline a sequel to the book.
i Write about an experience you have had which was similar to an incident in the story.
j Tell the story with you as protagonist. In what ways would you have reacted differently to the events?
k A friend of yours has written asking about the book. Write a letter back saying what you enjoyed most and least about it.
l Write up a major event in the book as a news item for a tabloid newspaper.
m Write a report for the police about a crime in the story.
n Write to the author of the book asking for clarification of a few things in the plot that you did not understand.

o Imagine you are directing a film of the book. What changes
might you make to the story and which actors would you
cast?

VARIATION 1

Student B reads the last chapter of A's book and vice versa,
rather than waiting for each other to read and summarize. B then
tells A to what extent the characters, storyline, atmosphere,
writing, etc. matched his or her expectations.

VARIATION 2

With lower levels, stages 1–6 are a useful way of encouraging
students to think about what they read.

COMMENTS

1 Explain to the class that they can improve not just their
reading but also other language skills—such as essay writing,
summarizing, and oral discussion—if they study a set book for
the exam.

2 For further ideas, see *Class Readers* by Jean Greenwood, in this
series.

Answers

3.5 b); e, f, c, a, b, d.

3.8 1 In a society where   2 not just . . . but   3 There is no
doubt that . . .   4 To some extent   5 simply because
6 While this may   7 even if   8 What is not so clear is
9 If . . . is anything to go by   10 likely to be

4 Grammar

This chapter consists of activities designed to prepare students for examination papers such as 'Use of English', 'Structure and Written Expression', 'English in Use', 'Grammar', 'Linguistic Tests', 'Knowledge of the English Language', and 'English Usage'.

These papers test students' knowledge of the language system, particularly grammatical aspects but in certain cases—such as Cambridge FCE, CPE, and MELAB—also vocabulary. Some exams, for example TOEFL, assess recognition of structural points while others, including Cambridge CAE, require candidates to show their ability to apply their knowledge of structure by completing tasks.

Students will find they need to study a wide range of structures if they are to be able to handle this part of the exam well, so you should advise students on how to use their grammar book. They should be familiar with the organization of the book, be able to use the index and—most importantly—understand the terminology used, so that for example they know they will find *the* under *definite article*. This chapter encourages students to think about grammatical expressions, particularly in 4.4, 4.10, and 4.13 (see also 2.15).

In addition, students will probably have to familiarize themselves with a number of different task types (see 1.3), often discrete-point exercises such as transformations or multiple choice. Great care needs to be taken in reading and following the instructions: help with this is given in 4.1 and in Chapter 1 (see 1.5, 1.6). With a variety of task types there is always a risk that students will get stuck on one of them, so you may want to advise them to start with those they find easiest—always assuming of course that exam regulations permit this. Suggestions for improving timing when doing these kinds of exercises is given in 1.10.

All the main task types of the principal exams are covered. Some of the activities (4.8, 4.9, 4.10) are equally valid for all the discrete-point types of exam question, while others concentrate on the most commonly used kinds of task. The 'open' cloze test (one-word gap fill) used in Cambridge FCE, CAE, and CPE, IELTS and ICC is the main focus of 4.1, 4.2, and 4.3, whereas 4.11 and 4.12 concentrate on the multiple-choice cloze seen in PET, FCE, CAE, MELAB, Oxford-Arels Preliminary, and Trinity. For more practice with cloze, see 2.1 and 2.12. Blank completion—filling in a missing word or phrase in a sentence, as in Cambridge CPE—is in 4.9 and 4.10, while filling gaps in questions (Trinity) is highlighted in 4.7 and practised in 4.10.

The three kinds of sentence transformation—rewriting using a prompt (CPE), re-writing beginning with a prompt (CPE and PET), and re-writing using both these prompts (FCE)—are practised in 4.6, 4.8, 4.9, and 4.10 (see also 4.13). Word formation (FCE) is the focus of 4.13; single-sentence multiple-choice questions, as used in CPE, are featured in 4.8 and 4.11; and written expression questions—as in TOEFL—in 4.10. Some of the exams—for example FCE and CPE, MELAB—also text lexical knowledge, therefore 4.14 looks at false cognates. For more vocabulary-building exercises, see Chapter 2, 'Reading'.

Doing lots of exam style grammar exercises does not necessarily mean that the students will learn the grammar they need. Practising cloze tests or sentence transformations, for example, may be useful in terms of familiarizing learners with the task, but if these are done on a hit-or-miss basis—without any consideration of why answers are right or wrong—there is unlikely to be a corresponding development in their command of structure.

For this reason the activities in this chapter also aim to build the students' knowledge of structures and their capacity to use them, as in activities 4.6, 4.8, and 4.10. Specific grammar areas featured include prepositions (4.1), *wish* (4.9), conditional forms (4.9), *it's time* + past tense (4.10), and prefixes and suffixes (4.13). There are also ideas for exploiting the grammar in exam instructions (4.1) and in exam-style exercises themselves. Students are encouraged to spot and correct spoken errors in 4.5, while 4.4 prepares learners for the proof-reading activity in FCE and CAE.

Other activities which should make the process of preparing for grammar tests less painful include providing clues to the answers (4.2), changing the questions to relate to the learner's own world (4.8), and adapting grammar exercises for use in teaching situations where there are different levels in one class (4.9).

4.1 Prepositions in instructions

LEVEL

Elementary and above

AIMS

To encourage careful reading of instructions; to focus on the use of prepositions; to practise filling gaps in texts

TIME

30 minutes

PREPARATION

1 At the beginning of the course, choose an exam paper which has extensive instructions.
2 Take out the prepositions and adverb particles, numbering the gaps, and make a list of them in jumbled order.

Example

Fill in each of the gaps with one of these words. Each word can be used more than once.

at   for   in   of   on   to

INSTRUCTIONS ___ (1) CANDIDATES

Write your name, Centre number and candidate number ___ (2) the spaces ___ (3) the top ___ (4) this page and ___ (5) the answer sheets unless this has already been done ___ (6) you.

This paper requires you to complete **all six tasks**.

___ (7) each question write your answer ___ (8) the **separate answer sheets**. Write clearly ___ (9) pen ___ (10) the numbered spaces provided.

NB Answers 81–88 must be written ___ (11) the back of Answer Sheet Two.

You may write ___ (12) the question paper if you wish, but you must **transfer your answers ___ (13) the separate answer sheets** within the time limit.

___ (14) the end of the examination you should hand ___ (15) both the question paper and the answer sheets.

INFORMATION ___ (16) CANDIDATES

The total number ___ (17) questions ___ (18) tasks 1 to 5 is 59; the last task is numbered 81–88. You do not need to write anything ___ (19) boxes 60 to 80 ___ (20) the answer sheet.

(*Cambridge Certificate in Advanced English*)

3 Give individuals, pairs, or groups a copy of the exam paper plus any separate answer sheets, or else make OHP transparencies.

PROCEDURE

1 Students fill in the gaps.

2 Check that everyone has the right answers (see key at end of chapter).

3 As a class, go through the exam paper and answer sheets. Students fill in example details and answers. Where the instructions use prepositions of place, for example *in* the spaces, *at* the top, *on* the answer sheets, they write them alongside:

Candidate Number	5736	in

Ask concept questions about the missing words. For example:

> **6** Do you always have to write your name? Why not? What is the difference, here, between *for* and *by*?
>
> **9** Can you write in pencil? What must you use?
>
> **13** If you write your answers on the question paper, what must you do? When?
>
> **15** Can you keep the question paper? What must you do with the question paper and the answer sheets?

COMMENTS

Remind students how essential it is to read and follow instructions carefully, and point out their extensive use of prepositions and adverb particles. You might also want to mention the fact that instructions can be a useful source of prepositions for checking answers!

4.2 Cloze clues

LEVEL

Elementary and above

AIMS

To develop cloze test skills

TIME

20 minutes; this activity is best done early on in the course

PREPARATION

1 Choose a suitable gap-fill text and divide it into three parts:
- for part (a), write the correct answers in jumbled order above the text;
- for part (b), write in part of the correct words in the gaps. This works best with gaps that need words of more than one syllable;
- for part (c), write just the initial letters into the gaps.

PROCEDURE

1 Students fill in the gaps.

2 In pairs or groups they compare answers and discuss the strategies they used in a), b), and c).

3 Check the answers (see key at end of chapter) and ask how students worked them out. Find out which clues helped them the most, and why/how.

Example

---

a Fill the gap with the correct word.
for   of   rather   in   which   what
A lot of the talk about the 'aging population' is nothing more than alarmist nonsense. The change involves an increase ___ (1) the average age of about two years, which will be virtually imperceptible. ___ (2) is often overlooked is the beneficial effect ___ (3) a more mature society in a developed economy, in ___ (4) there is a growing need ___ (5) highly qualified and experienced specialists ___ (6) than raw recruits to the workforce.

b Complete the missing words.
The young are far more expensive to *main*____ (1), in advanced societies, than the increasingly self-supporting old. Medical care, ____ *fare* (2) payments, council housing, education and the legal ____ *tem* (3)—a very high *prop*____ (4) of offenders are *juv*____ (5)—are all used disproportionately by the young, who contribute nothing in ____ *turn* (6).

c Complete the missing words.
The retired, on the other *h*____ (1) are often property owners *w*____ (2) private health and pension schemes *w*____ (3) do not exactly place a burden *o*____ (4) police resources, the courts, and the prison service. *I*____ (5) an age of mass unemployment we *s*____ (6) be grateful that fewer people are coming on to the jobs market.

Photocopiable © Oxford University Press

COMMENTS

Cloze tests can initially be very off-putting to students if their scores are consistently low, but they do become easier with practice if at first there are clues to guide readers to the right answers. Being able to fill in more of the gaps makes overall comprehension of the text easier and helps build confidence, as does getting to know the kinds of words and common collocations (juxtapositions of words) that are required. Take into account the students' comments from Procedure 3 above when deciding which kind of clues to use in future.

4.3 Making gaps

LEVEL

Intermediate and above

AIMS

To create student-generated cloze tests

TIME

25 minutes

PREPARATION

Find two authentic tests of around 200–250 words (they could be longer for higher levels or shorter for lower ones, but they must be complete). Look for easy-to-read newspaper or magazine articles on topics of interest to students, possibly in coursebooks. Make sets of copies of both texts.

PROCEDURE

1 Work through cloze exercises in the students' books that they have already done, getting the class to comment on the parts of speech most often required. In many cases these are prepositions, verb forms, and linking words. Choose a few examples and elicit the contextual clues that guide the reader to the right answers.

2 Students work in pairs with the texts you have prepared. Give Student A two copies of one test and Student B two copies of the other.

3 For homework, they blank or cut out 10, 15, or 20 words (the number depends on their level and experience with this activity)—particularly the kinds mentioned in stage 2—from one of the copies.

4 Students swap their gapped texts with each other and fill in as many gaps as they can.

5 They mark each other's work using the copy of the original, checking alternative answers with you.

COMMENTS

1 Explain to the class that designing cloze tests for each other is the best possible way of gaining an insight into how these exercises work. Point out that what is being tested is the ability to use the whole text for clues, not just the words next to the gaps.

2 The words chosen can provide you with useful feedback on what learners themselves regard as difficult. For example if they repeatedly delete *could*, *should*, and *may*, it might indicate that remedial work on modals is needed.

3 There may at first be a tendency for students to delete words such as adjectives and adverbs that are not essential to the meaning of the text as a whole. They might be relieved to learn that modern ELT exams are not about testing knowledge of obscure words.

4.4 Clues to mistakes

LEVEL

Lower-intermediate and above

AIMS

To identify error-correction items; to encourage the use of a correction code in essays; to practise intensive reading

TIME

30 minutes

PREPARATION

1 Look at the correction code in the Introduction (page 8) and take it a stage further by subdividing 'Grammar' to use a code consisting of, for example, vf = verb form, prep = preposition, art = article, adj = adjective, c/u = countable/ uncountable, mod = modal, adv = adverb, conj = conjunction, rel = relative clause, n = noun, pn = pronoun, neg = negative, q = question.

2 Select an error-correction text from past papers or practice tests. Alternatively, write your own text including mistakes your students often make. Write the code letters at the end of the lines that have mistakes in them. Make copies for the class or prepare it for the OHP.

3 Make copies of a suitable authentic paragraph, or choose one from the students' coursebook.

PROCEDURE

1 Students use the code as a guide to the type of error they must find. They either note the incorrect word down at the end of the line or write out a correct version of the text, depending on the format of the exam they are preparing for. Go over the answers with the class.

2 Hand out the authentic text and tell students to rewrite a paragraph from it, making a maximum of one deliberate exam-type mistake per line. If they can, they put the appropriate code letters at the end of the line.

3 Students exchange texts with their partners and find the mistakes.

Example

> **HOLISTIC TEACHING**
>
> The right and left hemispheres of the brain have quite different functions.
> The left brain is responsible of logic, analysis and the linear processing   prep
> of informations; the right brain for imagination, creativity, intuition, and   c/u
> the artistic appreciation. Most people have a natural preference towards   art
> (5) to use one or the other hemisphere. They will learn best if information is   vf
> presenting to them in a way which respects this preference. Teachers   vf
> which recognize this present their material in a way which is both logical   rel
> and analytical, imaginative, and artistic, so as both types of learner can   conj
> learn in the way what is most appropriate for them.   rel

(Lawlor 1993)

FOLLOW-UP 1   In the next lesson, students go through each other's homework and use the correction code to guide their partners to mistakes. They then correct their own work. Collect in and check the homework task, the correction code, and the students' corrections.

FOLLOW-UP 2   For higher levels, collect together examples of less-than-perfect English from tourist guides, signs, instruction manuals, etc. Get the class to identify and correct the mistakes, then tell them to find more examples.

COMMENTS   1 Remind the class of the value to the learning process of self-correction: that they are far more likely to learn from their mistakes if they have to identify them, think about them, and correct them for themselves. Explain that they will be integrating this into their preparation for the exam task.

2 Point out the potential practical applications of becoming skilled at spotting and correcting mistakes, for example working as proofreaders for firms, organizations, or institutions that produce documents in English, in their own countries or abroad. Error correction as a testing device can have quite a positive 'wash forward' effect.

4.5 Listening for mistakes

LEVEL

Elementary and above

AIMS

To practice error correction, reading aloud, and intensive listening

TIME

30 minutes

PREPARATION

None.

PROCEDURE

1 Divide the class into two teams, explain how the activity works, and ask each student to prepare at least one short sentence of the kind found in the exam error-correction task. Half the members of the team are to write sentences that are correct while the others must each write a sentence that contains a single grammatical error such as the incorrect use of the article, the wrong verb tense, confused singular/plural, inappropriate preposition, and so on. Errors which may not be easy for listeners to spot—leaving out the final /d/ of some past participles, for example—should be avoided.

2 A student from team A reads out a sentence. Team B has to decide whether there is a mistake and, if so, what the correct form should be.

3 Team B is awarded two points for identifying and correcting the mistake, and one point for correctly stating that there are no mistakes. They lose a point if they wrongly identify a form as being incorrect.

4 A student from team B reads out a sentence. Team A listens and, if necessary, corrects.

5 When all students have taken their turns the team with the most points is the winner.

4.6 Transformation pairs

LEVEL

Elementary and above

AIMS

To practise recognition and control of structures frequently tested in sentence-transformation exercises

TIME

30 minutes +

PREPARATION

1 On a worksheet or OHP transparency, make a list of transformation questions that the class have already done, in each case underlining the words which change from question to answer. Ignore any that have more than one grammatical change. (See Worksheet 1.)

2 On another worksheet, the OHP, or the board, put the structures into two columns: those from questions on the left, those from answers on the right, both in random order. (See Worksheet 2.)

Example

WORKSHEET 1

It's a pity they didn't come to the party.
wish
I wish they had come to the party.

That village is so lovely that everyone wants to live there.
such
It is such a lovely village that everyone wants to live there.

You don't have to bring any money with you.
need
There's no need for you to bring any money with you.

He doesn't play in the team any more.
used
He used to play in the team.

I've never done this before.
time
It's the first time I've done this.

I suggest you try again.
were
If I were you I'd try again.

(*Cambridge First Certificate in English, Revised 1996*)

WORKSHEET 2

it's a pity ... didn't	used to
I've never ... before	it is such a
don't have to	if I were you I'd
that ... is so	it's the first time I've
I suggest	I wish ... had
doesn't ... any more	there's no need for ... to

PROCEDURE

1 Put an example such as one of the sentences in Worksheet 1 on the board or OHP. Point out how certain structures tend to go together in transformation exercises.

2 The class study Worksheet 2 and match the pairs.

3 They check their answers by looking at the structures in the context of the original sentences in Worksheet 1.

4 Students go through the transformation questions in past papers or practice tests which they have already done, highlighting the pairs of structures as in the examples above. This could be done competitively or co-operatively, in pairs or groups.

5 Get the class to write more examples of their own using the same structures.

<table>
<tr><td>VARIATIONS</td><td>The principle is the same for other kinds of transformation item:</td></tr>
</table>

> She loves books <u>like that</u>.
> She loves <u>that</u> *kind of book*.

> <u>If you don't</u> switch it off it'll break!
> **else**
> *Switch it off <u>or else</u> it'll break*!

Also with lower levels:

> <u>I have a</u> red bicycle.
> <u>My</u> *bicycle* <u>is</u> *red*.

> The room <u>has</u> four windows.
> <u>There</u> *are four windows* <u>in</u> *the room*.

FOLLOW-UP   During future exam practice, students make a note of other pairs they come across and write examples.

COMMENTS   Point out that languages contain a huge number of lexical items but far fewer structures, so the same grammar points tend to recur in transformation exercises—frequently as matching pairs. Students who can spot these patterns often have the advantage of working with familiar changes when they do this kind of exam question.

4.7 Gaps in free-response questions

LEVEL   **Intermediate and above**

AIMS   **To practise completing gapped questions, answering free response questions, and reading for main points**

TIME   **15 minutes**

PREPARATION   **1** Choose a reading comprehension text with relatively simple questions requiring students to answer in their own words.

2 Delete two separate words in each question (if not already done as part of the exam task).

3 Jumble the missing words in a list.

PROCEDURE

1 Students read the text and complete the questions using the words from the list.

2 They answer the questions in their own words.

3 Pairs compare their questions and answers.

4 Collect in both questions and answers and check (see key at end of chapter).

Example

Put each of these words into one of the spaces in questions 1–5 below:
to   in   on   do   take   find   did   have   it   hit

Section A (20 marks)

Read the following passage. In the answer booklet write down the words to complete the questions at the end of the passage. Only TWO words are missing in each question. Then answer the questions.

Railway accidents are an unfortunate fact of life and the newspapers are always ready, with their dramatic stories and their pictures, to tell you all the horrific details.

But one of the most bizarre accidents happened recently in Bangladesh, when a local train ran into a baby elephant as it was trying to cross the line to reach its mother. Fortunately, the elephant was more alarmed than hurt but it quite naturally made a great deal of noise. This resulted in the enraged mother turning her attention on the train which she obviously regarded as guilty of an assault on her baby.

To the horror of the passengers, she attacked the train and damaged it so badly that it was unable to continue its journey. When she was satisfied with her work, she went off with her baby, leaving the unfortunate passengers to wait nearly five hours for a replacement train.

1 Why is — that newspapers — accidents so interesting?
2 — which country did this accident — place?
3 What was the baby elephant trying to — when it was — by the train?
4 How — the mother elephant react — the accident?
5 Did this incident — any effect — the passengers, if so what?

(*Trinity College London, ESOL Intermediate*)

(Note that candidates taking the Trinity College Intermediate examination will not be required to do this gap-filling exercise.)

VARIATION

With advanced classes, reduce some of the questions to note form:

3 What/baby/trying/when/hit/train?
4 How/mother/react/accident?

Students expand the notes to form complete questions, then answer them in their own words.

4.8 Personalizing the questions

LEVEL   **Lower-intermediate and above**

AIMS   **To reinforce knowledge and control of structure when doing discrete-point questions such as sentence transformation and multiple choice**

TIME   **30 minutes**

PREPARATION   Choose 20 sentence-level grammar questions from past papers or practice tests.

PROCEDURE   1 Students work in pairs. Each writes the answers to ten questions without letting their partner see the sentences.

2 Check the answers.

3 Students rewrite the questions—and the answers required—to reflect their own world. 'He' can become 'she' and vice versa. Instead of anonymous *they*'s or unknown *John*s and *Susan*s they use the name of fellow students, the teacher, friends, relatives, or famous people. They can change words to make the sentences more relevant, informative, or (perhaps best of all) funny. Anything, in fact, that makes sense, does not alter the structure being tested, and helps the student remember it.

4 Students complete each other's questions.

5 Students compare answers.

6 Ask for volunteers to read out some of their questions and get the rest of the class to answer them.

7 Collect in the other questions and answers, and check.

Example 1

Choose the word or phrase which best completes the sentence.

Employees do not like ..... by their boss when they have made a mistake.
A be corrected   C to correct
B correcting   D being corrected

Answer: *D*

Student A writes:
I don't like ..... by the teacher when I know I've made a mistake.
A being corrected   C correcting
B to correct   D be corrected

Student B writes: *A*

Example 2

> *Finish the following sentence in such a way that it is as similar as possible in meaning to the sentence printed before it.*
>
> Tom lost his job because he broke so many plates.
> If Tom ...
> Answer: If Tom *had not broken so many plates he would not have lost his job.*
>
> Student A writes:
> The Prime Minister lost his job because he broke so many promises.
> If the Prime Minister ...
>
> Student B writes:
> If the Prime Minister *had not broken so many promises he would not have lost his job.*

COMMENTS

Point out to the class that they are more likely to be able to learn structures if the context in which they occur is made more memorable.

4.9 Exercises for mixed levels

LEVEL

Lower-intermediate and above

AIMS

To practise discrete-point grammar questions at varying levels

TIME

15 minutes per question

PREPARATION

1 From past papers or practice tests, choose questions which focus on grammar points that have a variety of forms, for example reported speech, the passive, and the infinitive.

2 On a worksheet, the board, or OHP, write a number of alternative questions using the same structure, starting with easier ones and increasing the level of difficulty to a point where only a few in the class will be able to answer them.

3 Make sure everyone has access to a good grammar book.

PROCEDURE

1 Put the class into groups. Each should include an approximate balance of weak, average, and strong students.

2 Individual students write as many answers as possible. Those who finish first check their answers in the grammar book and make a note of the page references.

3 The stronger students tell the weaker ones where to find the information they need to answer the questions they could not do.

4 Check the answers. Ask groups which grammar points caused most difficulty and use the feedback as a basis for revision and/or remedial grammar work.

Example

In each exercise, complete as many of the sentences as you can. When you finish, note down the page number from your grammar book after each answer.

1 *Fill each of the blanks with a suitable word or phrase.*
  a I wish ___ live in a house like that.   (page 32)
  b I wish ___ money to buy that dress.   (page 32)
  c I wish ___ then what I know now.   (page 33)
  d I wish ___ live so far away.   (page 66)
  e I wish ___ keep making that awful noise.   (page 67)
  f I wish ___ deliver this message. Then you must
  return here.   (page 98)

2 *For questions (a)–(f), complete the second sentence so that it has a similar meaning to the first sentence, using the word given. Do not change the word given. You must use between two and five words, including the word given.*

They would never have succeeded if she had not helped.
HELP
  a Without ___ they would never have succeeded.   (page 44)
  b If she ___ they would never have succeeded.   (page 44)
  c Had she ___ they would never have succeeded.   (page 73)
  d But for ___ they would never have succeeded.   (page 86)
  e If it had not ___ they would never have
  succeeded.   (page 86)
  f Had it ___ they would never have succeeded.   (page 87)

Photocopiable © Oxford University Press

COMMENTS   Many tasks are easy to adapt for classes of mixed levels of skill. With reading or listening comprehension exercises, for example, add some easier and/or harder questions so that everyone can work to the maximum of their ability.

4.10 Grammar search

LEVEL

Elementary and above

AIMS

To reinforce grammar input by using discrete-point questions; to practise scanning texts for specific structures

TIME

30 minutes, plus 15 minutes in the next lesson

PREPARATION

When presenting, practising, or revising a given structure, find as many examples of it as you can in a book of practice tests. Ideally (but not essentially) the examples would be in various types of exercise.

PROCEDURE

1 Incorporate a few of the exam questions into the grammar work. Point out how they test knowledge of grammar patterns.

2 Direct the students to the rest of the examples in the practice test book. They answer the questions. Check their answers.

3 Students copy the questions and answers into their grammar notebooks. This gives them both further contexts for the grammar point as well as indicating which exam tasks are used to test it.

4 For homework, students find as many more examples of the structure as they can. Suggest they look at exercises already done, past papers, and other practice test books. Students answer them (again if necessary) and make a note of them as above.

5 In the next lesson students show their partners, or others in their group, the examples they have found. They answer them and note them down.

6 Collect in their work and check both questions and answers (see key at end of chapter).

VARIATION

Some of these types of question can also be used to focus on vocabulary areas. For example, collocations of *to do* (well, an exam, homework, etc.) or *to make* (mistakes, love, a noise, etc.).

Example

Structure: comparative adjectives

1 Their books are much ___ ours. (new)   (comparative + *than*)

2 mice/than/quickly/can/cats/run/more   (correct order)

3 Smith arrived late. The boss arrived later.   (one sentence)

4 The Pacific is more bigger than the Atlantic.   (remove word)

5 The train is more expensive than the bus.
   The bus ___   (same meaning)

6 My teacher is a better ___.   (finish)

Structure: *it's time* + past tense

1 It's time we ___ going if we're hoping to catch that train.
   A have   B were   C be   D are   (A,B,C, or D?)

2 You really shouldn't still be living in that dreadful place.
   It's ___ that dreadful place.   (2 to 5 words)

3 It's high time ___ her just what he's up to.
                                                    (word or phrase)

4 ... so it is obviously time we (6) ___ another look at the
   situation, unless ...   (1 word)

5 It's about ___ we left, but we'll be ___ touch soon.
                                                   (1 word in each)

6 Nobody can <u>any</u> (a) longer doubt that it is time we <u>begin</u> (b) to
   look <u>for</u> (c) an alternative source <u>of</u> (d) energy.
                                      (Which is incorrect: a,b,c, or d?)

Photocopiable © Oxford University Press

4.11 Defining options

LEVEL

Intermediate and above

AIMS

To focus on the nature of distractors, match definitions to words, and practise answering multiple-choice vocabulary questions

TIME

10–30 minutes, depending on the number of questions set

PREPARATION

1 Early on in the course, choose a number of vocabulary questions from past papers or a practice test book. If the latter, check that it does not use rare or non-occurring words as distractors. This activity should help students learn useful vocabulary, not waste time on obscure terms or expose learners to incorrect forms.

2 For each question, write a list of dictionary definitions for all the options, but in jumbled order. Ensure that these definitions refer to the way the words are used in the text and that they clearly distinguish between the four options.

PROCEDURE

1 The students match the definitions to the words.
2 They choose the correct answer to the question.

Example

Match definitions 1–4 with words A–D, then choose one of the words to fit the space

1 money paid for the release of a captive
2 sum of money offered for the capture of a criminal
3 written statement that something has been received
4 something given to the winner of a competition, race, etc.

A receipt   B prize   C ransom   D reward

Which word—A, B, C, or D—best fits the space?

According to a local radio station a ___ of $10,000 will be paid for information leading to the arrest of thieves who last night . . .

Photocopiable © Oxford University Press

VARIATION

In Preparation 2, get the students themselves to find the definitions, possibly for homework. Put the class into pairs and assign half of the questions to Student A, the other half to Student B. In the next lesson students ask their partners to match the definitions to the words.

COMMENTS

This is an activity for early on in the course. Stress the importance of deciding *why* multiple-choice distractors are wrong, and the potential for vocabulary-building which this provides if students are given (or find) a definition for each.

4.12 Adding a distractor

LEVEL

Upper-intermediate and above

AIMS

To focus on grammar and vocabulary items in multiple-choice cloze tests

TIME

30 minutes

PREPARATION

1 Take a cloze test accompanied by four-option one-word multiple-choice questions. The length of the text and the number of items will depend on the level of the class.

2 Blank out one of the distractors from each question. Make a list of these extra words, in random order, on the board or OHP.

Example

a *Read the text below and decide which word A, B, or C best fits each of the spaces 1–15*

BIKING TO HOSPITAL

American doctors have just put a question (1)___ against mountain-biking. (2)___ all the cyclists interviewed by one Californian doctor had suffered at least one injury in the (3)___ twelve months. Dr Robert Kronisch, a sports medicine consultant in San José who (4)___ completed a study of serious mountain biking injuries, discovered an incidence of damage (5)___ higher than for jogging or most other sports. Interviewing 265 (6)___, he found that 20 per cent had suffered injuries serious enough to warrant medical (7)___ in the last year.

(8)___ of the injuries were fractures, lacerations, and shoulder injuries, Dr Kronisch (9)___. Many of his interviewees for the Clinical Journal of Sports Medicine were from US mountain bike clubs, more (10)___ to take their machines over punishing terrain than (11)___. On the other (12)___, as (13)___ of a club, they are more likely to be (14)___ and to know their limits: beginners may be at more (15)___ of injury.

The Independent

	A	*B*	*C*	*Missing distractor*
1	sign	indicator	mark	_____
2	just	almost	about	_____
3	past	latest	recent	_____
4	formerly	recently	now	_____
5	yet	plenty	far	_____
6	riders	pilots	drivers	_____
7	attention	remedy	healing	_____
8	majority	amount	most	_____
9	informed	quoted	reported	_____
10	tending	likely	possible	_____
11	novices	recruits	pupils	_____
12	part	foot	hand	_____
13	mates	partners	members	_____
14	veteran	knowing	experienced	_____
15	hazard	jeopardy	risk	_____

b *Now look at questions 1–15 again. In each case choose the missing distractor from the list below and write it alongside the question above. Why is the missing distractor not correct?*

much	after	peril	conceivable	point
starters	elements	matured	hardly	cheek
presently	many	joyriders	denounced	restoration

PROCEDURE

1 Explain to the class that a 'distractor' is a possible answer which looks correct but is wrong.

2 Students fill in each of the gaps by choosing from its three remaining options.

3 Check the answers and ask why some of the distractors are wrong (see key at end of chapter).

4 Students match the extra distractors in the list on the board to the three options in each question. Check and ask them how they decided in each case.

VARIATION 1

Instead of deleting distractors from 1–15 think of a plausible *extra* distractor for each question and put a random-order list on the board for example:

side	already	colleagues	danger	over
experimented	quantity	signal	apprentices	very
ultimate	probable	conductors	cure	told

Students fill in the gaps. Check their answers. Then students match the words on the board to the questions. Ask them to explain their decisions.

VARIATION 2

In groups, the class fill in the gaps in a text and then think up a fifth, plausible but incorrect, option for each of the questions. Tell them they must be prepared to say why they chose the words and why they are wrong.

COMMENTS

1 Explain to the class that they are learning how multiple-choice questions work by studying the wrong answers—the distractors—and how they differ from the correct answers.

2 Speakers of some languages may suggest false cognates (English words which look like words in their first language but in fact have quite different meanings), thus showing awareness of their potential for error.

4.13 Forming words

LEVEL

Intermediate and above

AIMS

To practise word-formation exercises by identifying parts of speech and adding affixes

TIME

45 minutes

PREPARATION

Select a word-formation exercise from past papers or practice tests and a suitable reading comprehension text from the coursebook.

PROCEDURE

1 Tell the class that they will be learning how to use affixes and parts of speech as clues when doing word-formation exercises.

2 Put the first few lines of the exercise on the board or OHP and elicit the answers:

Union members are clearly (1) ___ about a broad   HAPPY
range of issues, above all the (2) ___ by management to ...   REFUSE

3 Elicit the part of speech of both the answer and word in capitals. Write this in next to each word. If the affix gives the word a negative meaning, note this as well:

Union members are clearly (1) *unhappy* [adj, neg] about a broad
                                                            HAPPY [adj]

range of issues, above all the (2) *refusal* [n] by management to ...
                                                            REFUSE [v]

4 The class do the same with the rest of the exercise. Check their answers.

5 Focus on the comprehension text and choose words which can be modified by adding affixes, such as *learn*, *success*, and *strong*. Ask the class what part of speech they are. In groups, students form as many words as they can from these 'stems', put *adj*, *adv*, *n*, or *v* next to each and report back to the class. For example:

... but nowadays nobody seems to <u>care</u> about the problem, much less want to ... care [v]; careful [adj], careless [adj, neg], carefully [adv], carelessly [adv, neg] carefulness [n], carelessness [n, neg], carer [n], caring [adj], etc.

6 Students search the text for words which have been modified in the same way and write the stems at the end of the lines, noting the parts of speech. Check. For example:

... using the cover of <u>darkness</u> [n] to stalk its prey, which consists ...
                                                            DARK [adj]

VARIATION

For more advanced classes, the first stage could be done for homework.

1 Put the class into pairs. Choose a suitable paragraph for all the Student As to work with and one from another text for the Bs. They re-write the paragraph with a maximum of one word per line left out and the stem written in capitals at the end of the line. To make the task easier they can put the part of speech required in brackets. For example:

Hundreds of (1) ___ [n] gathered on the site to protect against
                                                            DEMONSTRATE [v]

the planned (2) ___ [n] of the road, which campaigners   BUILD [v]

say is (3) ___ [adj, neg] and likely to have a devastating   NECESSARY [adj]

impact in an area famous for its (4) ___ [adj] scenery.   BEAUTY [n]

2 Students exchange paragraphs with their partners and fill in the gaps.

3 They check their answers against the original texts (see key at end of chapter).

4 Then they rewrite the phrases or sentences from the paragraph, using the stems (as in a transformation exercise). For example:

DEMONSTRATE	– hundreds of people gathered on the site to <u>demonstrate</u>
BUILD	– they were protesting against plans to <u>build</u> the road
NECESSARY	– campaigners say it is not <u>necessary</u>
BEAUTY	– famous for the <u>beauty</u> of its scenery

4.14 False friends

LEVEL

Intermediate and above

AIMS

To heighten awareness of false cognates, especially in multiple-choice vocabulary tasks; to practise dictionary use and matching definitions to words; to discuss and write definitions

TIME

60 minutes

PREPARATION

1 Remind speakers of certain languages, including Greek and languages of Latin or Germanic origin, that although there are many helpful cognates in English, there are some words that look the same but have quite different meanings, and that awareness of them is often tested in vocabulary sections of exams.

2 Ensure that everyone has a good English dictionary and knows how to use it.

3 Hand out sets of multiple-choice vocabulary questions, preferably from past papers. It does not matter if students have already done them.

PROCEDURE

1 Working individually, students look through all the options in each question, checking the meanings of those that look like words in their first language.

2 Students use these to make two lists: the definitions on the left and the words, in jumbled order, on the right. They keep a separate record of the question/test number for each word.

3 Tell students to keep looking up words until they have found a certain number of 'false friends' to include. This number can vary from just one or two expressions to all of them in the case of a very advanced class.

4 Students exchange lists and match the words with the definitions.

Example

> *Match the definitions on the left with the words on the right.*
>
> | | |
> |---|---|
> | to help | prediction |
> | to make something happen | sensible |
> | really; in fact; though it may seem strange | assist |
> | action of predicting; a forecast or prophesy | cause |
> | having or showing good sense; reasonable | opposition |
> | resistance, competitors or rivals | actually |

5 Students tell one another of other false cognates which they know, looking up the meanings where necessary.

6 After the definitions of the English words, students explain the meanings of the first language words. In some cases they may also be able to write a translation of the English false cognate. For example:

assist	=	to help (*ayudar*)
asistir	=	to attend
actually	=	really; in fact; though it may seem strange (*realmente; en efecto*)
actualmente	=	now; nowadays
sensible	=	having or showing good sense; reasonable (*prudente; sensato*)
sensible	=	sensitive

7 Encourage students to keep a special notebook for false friends, adding new ones as they come up during the course.

COMMENTS

If you have a good knowledge of the students' first language, guide them to some of the most confusing vocabulary items. If not, a useful source of false cognates is a native speaker of their language who is also an English teacher. See also *Learner English* by Michael Swan and Bernard Smith.

Answers

4.1

1 to	2 in	3 at	4 of
5 on	6 for	7 For	8 on
9 in	10 in	11 on	12 on
13 to	14 At	15 in	16 for
17 of	18 for	19 in	20 on

4.2 a)

1 in	2 what	3 of	4 which
5 for	6 rather		

b)

1 maintain	2 welfare	3 system	4 proportion
5 juveniles	6 return		

c)

1 hand	2 with	3 who	4 on
5 In	6 should		

4.7   1 it; find   2 in; take   3 do; hit   4 did; to
     5 have; on

4.9   1 a) I could   b) I had enoug
         c) I had known   d) they didn't
         e) they wouldn't   f) you to
      2 a) her help   b) had not helped them
         c) not helped them   d) her help
         e) been for her help   f) not been for her help

4.10 Comparatives: 1 newer than   2 cats can run more
     quickly than mice   3 the boss arrived later than Smith
     4 more   5 is cheaper than the train   6 ... than ...

     It's time: 1 B   2 time you left/moved out of
     3 you told her   4 took/had   5 time; in
     6 B is incorrect

4.12 b) 1 point   2 hardly   3 after
     4 presently   5 many   6 joyriders
     7 restoration   8 much   9 denounced
     10 conceivable   11 starters   12 cheek
     13 elements   14 matured   15 peril

     Variation: 1 signal   2 over
     3 ultimate   4 already   5 very
     6 conductors   7 cure   8 quantity
     9 told   10 probable   11 apprentices
     12 side   13 colleagues   14 experimented
     15 danger

4.13 Variation: 1 demonstrators   2 building
                3 unnecessary   4 beautiful

5 Listening

The activities in this chapter are intended to help students prepare for examination papers such as 'Listening Comprehension' and 'Listening'.

At lower levels candidates will be expected to understand gist, main points, and certain details, even if the text is too difficult to be understood completely. In Cambridge PET they will also need to be able to appreciate the speakers' attitudes and intentions. At higher levels, for example in Cambridge FCE, CAE, and CPE, TOEFL, Oxford-Arels, IELTS, IOL (PC, D), Trinity (10–12), and ICC (3), they must also understand other features such as mood, function, roles, location, relationship, opinions, emotions, or register. In addition candidates may be asked to infer meaning.

Except at the lowest levels, for example Cambridge KET, texts are presented at normal speaking speed and may include common non-standard accents. In some exams, such as Cambridge FCE, there may be non-native speakers. The speech on TOEFL recordings, however, is always that of standard North American English.

Background noise can make comprehension more difficult so at lower levels it is usually avoided, although it may be present in exams such as the Oxford-Arels Higher or Cambridge CCSE, which use source material recorded in authentic conditions: see 5.3. In some exams—this is often the case in the Cambridge listening comprehension—the recording is played twice, while in other exams candidates hear it only once, as in TOEFL and MELAB. It is recommended that users of this book follow the format of the target exam unless otherwise advised in the activity.

Most exams use a wide range of text types, so preparation should reflect this. Possibilities include announcements, advertisements, news items, conversations, interviews, telephone recorded messages, telephone dialogues, commentaries, stories, speeches, lectures, debates, studio discussions, quiz programmes, songs, or drama.

Several of the activities in this chapter (5.3, 5.6, 5.10, 5.12) can be used for just about any kind of exam listening task. Others concentrate on particular types of exercise, such as filling blanks or taking notes (5.1, 5.2, 5.4, 5.5, 5.9; see also 6.12), frequently used in all the Cambridge and Oxford-Arels exams. A particularly common variant of this task type entails studying a series of incomplete sentences on the question paper, listening for the parts of the text which these sentences paraphrase, and then filling in the missing words: in 5.9 students practise writing the incomplete sentences, not the missing words.

Answering multiple-choice questions—as in PET, FCE, and CPE, TOEFL, MELAB, and ICC—is a feature of 5.11 and 5.13 (see also 2.13), while true/false and yes/no questions, common in PET, FCE, and CPE, are dealt with in 5.7: here students find out how exam questions work by writing them for each other.

The different kinds of text most often used in exams are dealt with in separate activities, for example the short conversations like those in the first part of TOEFL (5.13) and the longer dialogues (5.14) or interviews of the type common in the higher-level Cambridge exams. Some exams—for example Cambridge CCSE and CAE, IOL and Oxford-Arels—require students to respond to what they have heard by writing a text. This is practised in 5.5 (see also 6.12). FCE, CAE, and CPE also use various types of matching and ordering question: 5.14 includes putting the main points in the order they are heard, while 5.6 and 5.16 focus on the multiple matching tasks featured in the 1996 revised FCE.

As candidates may need to understand not only what is said but how, and sometimes why, something is said (or, for that matter, not said), special attention is paid to focusing on the speakers' attitudes and inferring what they mean, particularly in activities 5.8 and 5.13. The recording may then be used as a model for students to work on their speaking skills, as in 5.13 and 5.14.

A constant aim in this chapter is to build up the learners' confidence so that they do not feel overwhelmed by the torrent of language from the recording. Activities help to make the task more manageable by helping learners to decide what kinds of answer are needed (5.1), decide quickly what kind of text they are listening to (5.3), and rapidly assimilate the main points (5.2, 5.14, see also 6.5). Activity 5.5 gives practice with the difficult task of simultaneous listening and writing, while 5.10 focuses on identifying language features such as topic, context, function, and register—especially useful for the Cambridge exams from PET upwards. Students may also encounter difficulties if there are rapid changes of situation, as in the revised Cambridge FCE. Activity 5.3 should help with this.

Another main objective is to reduce the load when students listen: students predict what they will hear by studying the written instructions, the questions, and any examples (5.4), by listening carefully to the spoken introduction (5.12), by thinking about the topic and the vocabulary they associate with it (5.6), and by putting themselves in the shoes of one of the speakers and imagining their interlocutor's responses (5.15).

5.1 Clues to blanks

LEVEL	**Elementary and above**
AIMS	**To develop confidence in writing blank completion answers while listening**
TIME	**10 minutes; best done at the start of the course**
PREPARATION	Choose a typical blank-filling exercise and, by listening to the tape or reading the transcript, design a one-word clue to each answer. This clue should help guide the student to the type of answer required.
PROCEDURE	1 Write the question numbers on the board or OHP and put the clues next to each.
	2 The class listen to the recording, refer to the clues, and fill in the answers.

Example

For each question, use the clue to help you answer:
9 (country)   10 (nationality)   11 (place)   12 (language)

(extract)

PART 2

You will hear part of a radio talk about a language course for British people.
For questions 9–18, complete the notes which summarize what the speaker says. You will need to write a word or a short phrase in each space.

Students on the course come from	9
Teachers are	10
Students previously studied at	11
Grammar lessons are in	12

(*Cambridge First Certificate in English*, Revised 1996)

VARIATION	Students look at the questions and for each one predict the kind of answer they should be listening for. Play the tape once so that they can check if their predictions were right, then a second time for them to write in their answers.

5.2 Establishing facts

LEVEL

Elementary and above

AIMS

To help students choose which main points and details to extract

TIME

30 minutes; this activity is best done at the beginning of the course

PREPARATION

1 Select a suitable listening comprehension passage from past papers or a book of practice tests.

2 Prepare worksheets with these three headings about the passage:
a) Things you know are true.
b) Things that might be true.
c) Things that you don't know.

PROCEDURE

1 Play the tape, leaving out the exam task instructions. Students note down 3–6 points under each heading, the number depending on the students' level and whether they listen once or twice. These could be basic facts such as a speaker's occupation and where a dialogue takes place, or they could be more abstract things such as someone feeling guilty about something.

2 After listening, the students form groups. They tell the others the points they have noted in category a), check those in category b), and ask about those in category c).

3 Ask the class which points they noted down in all three categories and discuss the answers.

4 Students listen again and do the exam task.

5 Go through the answers, asking the class in which category—a), b), or c)—they had placed the point corresponding to the exam answer. If there are any points relevant to the exam answers that they had not noted down, ask why.

5.3 Which text types?

LEVEL

Elementary and above

AIM

To identify text types in listening comprehension

TIME

45–60 minutes; this is an activity for the beginning of the course

PREPARATION

1 Collect together plenty of transcripts of listening comprehension texts from past papers.

2 Choose extracts from six very different types of text, for example a radio news item, in-flight information, a speech, an advertisement, instructions, one side of a phone conversation, and put them, numbered, on a worksheet. These extracts should be from near the beginning of the texts and contain clues to the type of text they come from.

3 Add a list of the six text types in jumbled order.

4 Have the complete transcripts ready for pairs or groups to use, as well as the recordings.

PROCEDURE

1 Working alone, students match the six extracts to the text types.

2 Students decide what the clues were in each case and highlight them in the text. These could include proper names, times, figures, verb forms, language functions, and register/style.

3 Put the class into pairs or groups. Students listen to the recordings and make a note of all the clues they hear. Then they check them against the complete transcripts.

4 Go through texts and clues as a class.

Example

---

1 ... so if you're in fairly soon you can call me back on 645 5080. I'll be here till around half past nine but then I've got to ...

2 ... and now the latest currency rates in New York: the dollar is 12 points weaker than Friday's close at 1.8732 marks and ...

3 ... but then with just 3 minutes to go Fowler left the entire United defence standing to score the goal that put ...

4 ... the next train to arrive at platform 12 is the 0745 to Paris Gare du Nord, calling at Lille only. Restaurant facilities are ...

5 ... where winds will be strong to gale force with scattered showers falling as sleet or snow over high ground, clearing later ...

6 ... 'cause you know what Grant would've done if he'd found out about him and Sharon, well I mean you saw him that time ...

A railway announcement
B weather forecast
C informal conversation
D financial report
E message on a telephone answering machine
F sports report

VARIATION 1   Students listen to short extracts from the recordings instead of
reading them. Ensure that the extracts are clearly numbered and
get the class to match them with the written list of text types
A–F. Extra points for discussion include background noise,
giving clues as to where someone is speaking; tone of voice,
showing the relationship between the speakers; and sound
quality, indicating whether what is heard is spoken on the phone,
over a public address system, or by a computer.

VARIATION 2   This activity can also be used with reading comprehension texts.

COMMENTS   Rapid identification of listening comprehension text type enables
students to picture the situation quickly and predict what they
are going to hear, both in terms of the content and the way it is
spoken.

5.4 Reading the questions

LEVEL   Intermediate and above

AIMS   To encourage careful study of the question paper before
note taking or blank filling; to practise predicting listening
input

TIME   30 minutes

PREPARATION   1 Choose two single-text listening tasks which require students
to fill in details on the question paper. The information already
given on the question paper should provide an outline of the
listening text.

2 For one of the tasks, prepare six questions about the main
points of the text, focusing on situation, gist, and certain details
so that a framework of what students will hear is created.

PROCEDURE   1 Focus attention on the information in the question paper, put
your questions on the board or OHP, and elicit the answers to
them.

2 Check the answers and then complete the exam task.

3 Students now study the question paper for the second
listening task and write their own questions about it.

4 Students exchange with their partners and write their answers.

5 Go through their questions and answers as a class before
doing the exam task.

Example

What kind of written text is this?
How many speakers do you think there will be?
Who are they?
How will they sound?
What kind of questions do you expect to hear?
What kinds of words and numbers do you need for the answers?

For each question, fill in the missing information in the numbered space.

RADIO 749 SHOP WINDOW

First caller – Isabel
Wants to sell a (**14**) _____
Paid £500, wants £200.
Size: (**15**) _____
Ring 491268

Second caller – Tony
Selling a (**16**) _____
Price: – around £65.
Address: 21 (**17**) _____
Call round after 6pm

Third caller – Ted
Wants to sell his (**18**) _____
Price: £340.
Colours: (**19**) _____
Ring 73155 any time

(Fried-Booth 1996)

VARIATION

For less advanced levels, it may at first be advisable to provide alternative answers to your questions for students to choose from.

COMMENTS

Point out to the class the value of being able to predict what they are going to hear before they actually listen to it, and the difficulty of reading and listening simultaneously. Remind them to ask themselves questions like the ones in this activity before doing future listening tasks.

5.5 Listen and write

LEVEL

Intermediate and above

AIMS

To practise listening for specific details, writing predictions in response to listening input, intensive reading, and oral discussion of predictions

TIME

45 minutes

PREPARATION

1 A week before the lesson, make a recording of a radio news item from an English-speaking country. It should be a 'rolling' story likely to develop over the next week, such as an attempt to break a record, a legal case, an election campaign, a scandal or other human interest story, preferably one that the students are unlikely otherwise to hear about.

2 Just before the lesson the latest developments are recorded. If this is not practicable, make a note of the details.

PROCEDURE

1 Students write Who/What/Where/When/How/Why headings in their notebooks.

2 They listen—twice if necessary—to the text from Preparation 1 above and write down the main points under each heading.

3 Mark the answers as in the listening part of the exam: probably one mark for each correct point.

4 Students use the data and their imagination to write an account of what they think will happen next in the story.

5 In pairs, students read their partners' texts and agree or disagree with their predictions.

6 Students listen to the latest news on the story—either on tape or from you—and add more points under the headings from stage 1. Give marks as in stage 3.

7 In pairs students discuss the accuracy of the predictions they made at stage 4.

VARIATION

The recording contains several news items: students fill in details under each heading in stage 1 on all of them. Check that students have noted the main points. Each learner then chooses one story and continues with stages 4 and 5.

5.6 Predicting vocabulary

LEVEL

Elementary and above

AIMS

To predict text vocabulary; to practise listening for specific words; to practise multiple matching

TIME

45 minutes

PREPARATION

1 Choose a listening comprehension text that has a clearly defined single topic.

2 Before the lesson, listen to the tape or read a transcript of it. As you do so, note down all the words associated with the topic. For example, if the subject is 'parachuting', you might pick out *jump, plane, danger, sky, speed, air, pull, open, ground, thrilling*.

PROCEDURE

1 Put the class into groups and tell them the topic of the text. Get them to write down 10, 20, or 30 content words they think will be used. You may wish to monitor the lists for spelling.

2 Groups exchange lists.

3 The class listen to the recording. Whenever students hear one of the words on the list in front of them they tick it.

4 Students make a note of any ticked words which they had not thought of and give the list back to the group that wrote it.

5 The class listen again and check their own list plus the new words from the other group's list.

6 As a class discuss any differences in the choice of words ticked. Ask which group correctly predicted most words.

7 Do the exam task and check the answers. Ask the class which of the words they predicted made the task easier, and how. Then collect in the lists of words to check.

VARIATION

This activity can also be adapted for use with the kind of multiple matching task below. Choose words related to the individual topics, for example *downstairs* in the case of place A below, and at stage 1 tell students to predict perhaps 5 or 6 expressions for each of the places A–F. Then proceed as in the main activity.

COMMENTS

Remind students to think about the vocabulary they might hear whenever they are about to do a listening task. This can help them recognize more of the text when they listen to it, and reinforce the vocabulary when they hear it used.

Example

You will hear five people talking about a place where they're living. For Questions 19–23, choose from the list of places A–F what each speaker is describing.

Use the letters only once. There is one extra letter which you do not need to use.

A a house	Speaker 1	19
B a flat	Speaker 2	20
C a caravan	Speaker 3	21
D a rented room	Speaker 4	22
E a hotel	Speaker 5	23
F a holiday cottage		

(*Cambridge First Certificate in English*, Revised 1996)

5.7 Writing dual-choice questions

LEVEL

Intermediate and above

AIMS

To practise extracting the main points of a text and writing true/false or yes/no questions about them

TIME

45 minutes

PREPARATION

Choose two exam-style true/false or yes/no listening tasks with texts which are easy to follow and contain plenty of facts. Set gist questions for the second text. Transcripts are useful but not essential.

PROCEDURE

1 Set the exam task and check the answers when students have finished.

2 Go through each of the questions, asking the class how they decided on their answers and which clues they used. Then point out more of the clues either in the recording or the transcript.

3 Set some simple gist listening questions for the second text. Don't let the students see the exam task. Play the recording to the class once and check their overall understanding from their answers to your gist questions.

4 Explain to the class that the next time they hear the text they are to write down six simple statements about it which are either clearly true or false. You may want them to include sentences about the speakers and their attitudes, as well as factual information. They should also make a note of the answers.

5 Play the recording again, pausing regularly for everyone to write their statements.

6 When listening and writing have finished, students answer sheets with their partners, who put T (true) or F (false) next to each sentence.

7 Students compare and discuss their answers with the students who wrote the questions, checking with you if they disagree on any items.

Example

Listening text: (extract)   ... but I'm afraid that Wednesday is our day off so it'll have to be another evening. How about Monday? It's always pretty quiet then and most of the courts are free, but I will have to check first with the manager, who should be back from lunch at around one thirty. So if you could ring back a little later I should be able to tell you ...

Examples of students' statements:

True (T) or False (F)?

They are closed on Wednesdays. ....

Mondays are very busy. ....

The manager is out. ....

VARIATION 1   Stages 1–5 as above, but instead of working in pairs everyone contributes one or two statements to a list on the board or OHP. The class then listen to the tape and decide whether the statements are true or false.

VARIATION 2   This activity also works well with reading comprehension texts.

5.8 Attitudes and feelings

LEVEL   **Lower-intermediate and above**

AIMS   **To practise inferring speakers' attitudes and feelings; to practise gist listening**

TIME   **30–45 minutes**

PREPARATION   1 Choose a recording of fairly emotional dialogue from a book of exam practice tests. Students will need a transcript which they can write on in pencil.

2 Make photocopies of a worksheet something like this one:

```
┌─────────────────────────────────────────────────────────────────┐
│                                                                   │
│   Situation?  _____  │
│                                                                   │
│   _____ │
│                                                                   │
│   Topic of conversation?  _____  │
│                                                                   │
│   _____ │
│                                                                   │
│   Speaker 1: Male or female? _____ Age? _____           │
│                                                                   │
│   Speaker 2: Male or female? _____ Age? _____           │
│                                                                   │
│   Relationship between speakers?* _____   │
│                                                                   │
│   *friends, couple, boss/employee, etc.                           │
│                                                                   │
└─────────────────────────────────────────────────────────────────┘
```

Photocopiable © Oxford University Press

PROCEDURE

1 Elicit adjectives of emotion, put them on the board, and check that everyone understands them. The list could include *happy, upset, irritated, hesitant, angry, sad, apologetic, bored, tired, amused, impatient, relaxed, threatening*; perhaps also *cynical, sympathetic, patronizing, sceptical, reassuring* with more advanced classes. If students do not suggest all of the adjectives needed for the activity, give prompts such as 'It's when you think something bad might happen' (worried) or 'It's when something happens which you didn't expect' (surprised).

2 Play the tape, leaving out recorded instructions such as 'tick one of the boxes'. Students complete the worksheet.

3 Discuss the answers with the class.

4 Play the recording again. This time students follow the transcript as they listen, underlining those sections where they can identify the expression of an attitude or emotion, and writing the appropriate adjective underneath. Suggest how students can recognize them. For example, a wide pitch range indicating a strong emotion such as impatience or surprise; a narrow pitch range showing boredom; a rising tone expressing doubt or curiosity; a falling tone when someone feels sure about something.

5 Students compare notes with their partners and then with the rest of the class.

6 Play the tape again, pausing where appropriate to focus on how the speaker feels.

Example

Politician: 'Now if you're suggesting that we should put up
                 interest rates in order to keep some artificial exchange
                 rate with a foreign currency whose economy <u>really
                 has very little to do with us</u> ...
                            amused

Presenter: 'I just think she's had a raw deal going on holiday,
                 <u>that's all</u> ...'
                 impatient

Questioner: 'Well I do think we get a raw deal, through this
                 government. I think it's <u>about time they were
                 kicked out.</u>'
                      angry

VARIATION

During the pauses on the third listening, students practise
sounding angry, hesitant, and so on by repeating the speakers'
words using the same stress and intonation patterns.

5.9 Completing statements

LEVEL

Intermediate and above

AIMS

**To focus on sentence-completion items in listening tasks;
to practise paraphrasing**

TIME

45 minutes

PREPARATION

1 Choose a sentence-completion task. The sentences should
summarize the main points of a text, as in the example below.

2 Make a worksheet, leaving out these sentences but putting the
missing words on the right. Prepare some gist questions about
the text. Transcripts would be useful but are not essential.

PROCEDURE

1 Put the gist questions on the board and play the tape once.
Elicit the answers.

2 Hand out the worksheet and tell students to look at the
'missing' words, explaining any difficult expressions.

3 Play the tape again, pausing before the last word in each
sentence. This time students use the 'missing' words as clues to
complete each sentence.

4 Play the tape for a third time to enable students to check their
sentences, or hand out transcripts.

5 Collect in their work and check.

Example

The final little piece of evidence related right back to the shooting. When the incident occurred the police had put out enquiries as to whether anyone had seen an old brown motorcycle. A man had come forward and said 'Yes, I saw this old brown motorcycle and he almost collided with me. In fact he had to swerve. As he swerved, a piece of cloth fell from the motorbike onto my car.' The police said 'Well where's that piece of cloth now?' and the driver said 'Well I was going to work and I put it on a wall inside the place I work.'

The police then go down to the man's work and the cloth is no longer on the wall. Where is it? Someone from inside the factory remembers using the cloth to wipe down machinery. Where is it now? 'I threw it into the waste bin.' Go along to the waste bin— and of course it's no longer there. The refuse collectors have been. This is where we all know of course that the use of police cadets comes in, because they searched the refuse tip and they found the piece of cloth.

And eventually that piece of cloth actually fitted back into the torn part of a blanket which was back in the suspect's home some forty miles away.

(transcript from *BBC World Service*)

Worksheet

Gist questions

1 *The police were investigating a* _____
2 *They wanted information about an* _____
3 *The motorcyclist had to* _____
4 *He dropped* _____
5 *The car driver took it* _____
6 *He put the cloth on* _____
7 *Someone used it to clean* _____
8 *Then he threw it into the* _____
9 *It was taken away by the* _____
10 *The police found it on a* _____
11 *It was part of* _____
12 *This belonged to the suspect, who lived* _____

'Missing words'

shooting   old brown motorcycle   swerve
a piece of cloth   to work   the wall   machinery
waste bin   refuse collectors   refuse tip   a blanket
40 miles away

5.10 Listening for specific language

LEVEL

Elementary and above

AIMS

To practise identifying language features—vocabulary, structure, function, or register—in comprehension texts

TIME

30 minutes

PREPARATION

Choose an exam listening text which deals with a single topic, uses one verb tense in particular, expresses a particular language function (praising or criticizing, for example) in a number of ways, or else is in a consistent style or register. Listen carefully to the text, or study a transcript.

PROCEDURE

1 The class listen once and identify one of the following: the vocabulary area, the most-used verb tense, a repeated function, the level of formality, or any other recurring feature such as the use of semi-specialist language.

2 They listen for a second time and note down all the words and phrases that are examples of (or supply) the information they are listening for. It may be advisable to pause the tape occasionally.

3 The class make a list of the expressions, possibly on the board or OHP.

4 Check that all the students understand the expressions, and why they are used in the text.

5 Students listen again and do the exam task, using the expressions as clues.

6 Check their answers.

Examples

VOCABULARY

What is the main topic of this extract?

'... Try to pick the time of day when you reach Paris. If you're likely to be coming into the city at anything even vaguely resembling a <u>rush hour</u>, stop for a meal at one of the excellent— and I'm not joking—<u>motorway</u> self-service restaurants and let the <u>traffic</u> subside a bit. Or, if you've had a long <u>drive</u> already, you could do worse than check into one of the many comfy but ultra-cheap <u>motels</u> dotted along the ...'

A meals in France   B hotels in France   C driving in France

VERB TENSE

Listen to this journalist talking about an evening newspaper. What can we infer about it?

... People <u>read</u> it so they <u>can</u> follow local stories and to find out what'<u>s</u> on, especially on TV, and often what the latest <u>is</u> on one of the three big football teams. When they <u>pick</u> it up they <u>may</u> be tired and <u>want</u> to relax after work, or else they'<u>re</u> on the bus or underground home, so they <u>don't want</u> to have to plough through anything too heavy ...'

A it is no longer published   B it is published every day
C it does not yet exist

FUNCTIONS

Listen to the mechanic talking over the phone to a motorist. Why is he speaking to her?

'... Well <u>I think the first thing to do</u> is check the tank. I know it's pretty obvious but you'd be amazed how often people just run out of petrol and don't realize it. Then <u>you should</u> have a look at the battery and if that's OK <u>it'd be a good idea</u> to check the fuses too. It's usually fuel or electrical so <u>you'd better</u> make sure there aren't any loose cables ...'

A to advise her   B to apologize to her   C to ask her opinion

REGISTER

Listen to this message at a hotel. What sort of language is used?

' ... Guests <u>are kindly requested</u> to use the waste-paper baskets provided and to <u>refrain from</u> smoking. Rooms should be <u>vacated</u> by eleven o'clock on the morning of <u>departure</u> and all keys <u>deposited</u> at reception. Thank you for your attention.'

A informal   B formal   C technical

5.11 In other words

LEVEL	**Elementary and above**
AIMS	**To reduce the vocabulary load in listening comprehension tasks—especially multiple-choice questions**
TIME	**30 minutes**
PREPARATION	1 From a listening comprehension text, make a note of all the expressions which can easily be put into other words. These should be words that your students already know or have seen recently.

2 Draw up two lists: list A has the original expressions from the text; list B contains your alternatives.

PROCEDURE

1 Read out the words in list A and elicit different ways of saying them.

2 Put the words from list B on the board or OHP, in jumbled order.

3 Students match the words from the two lists. Check their answers.

4 Students do the exam task.

Example

> … Welcome aboard our Boeing 737. We would ask you, for your comfort and safety, to comply with safety regulations: to place any hand luggage under the seat in front of you, or in the lockers overhead. Your hand luggage must not obstruct the aisles or emergency exits.
>
> We'll be coming through the cabin with landing cards: you do not require these cards if you're transferring directly to an international flight or if you've a European Community passport …
>
> **List A**
> comply with regulations   place   overhead   obstruct
> exits   require   transferring
>
> **List B**
> block   above   need   obey   rules   put
> changing   ways out

Photocopiable © Oxford University Press

VARIATION

With more advanced classes, note down the words which point to the right answer. These may be expressions that mean the same as, mean the opposite to, or have a misleadingly superficial similarity to certain words in the question.

1 The class do the exam task in the usual way. Check the answers.

2 Play the recording again. This time students note down the key words that led them to the correct answers. Play the recording again if necessary.

3 Students make a list of matching pairs of expressions from the text and questions, marking next to each whether the meanings are the same (S), the opposite (O), or likely to confuse (C).

Example

grew up	–	spent my childhood	(S)
every day of the year	–	365 days a year	(S)
up and down	–	vertically	(S)
are free	–	you have to pay	(O)
can't understand	–	totally unintelligible	(S)
affected	–	improved	(C)
resigned	–	dismissed	(O)

4 To follow up, study more past papers and make a worksheet list of matching expressions: the words in the questions on the left and, in jumbled order, those from the recording on the right. If transcripts are available, get the class to find as many matching pairs as they can.

Example

Match expressions in the column on the left with others on the right. Mark them S (same), O (opposite), or C (confusing).

S, O, or C?

starts	borrowed
events	begins
dull	afford
short of money	let's
buy	exciting
suggest	things coming up

Think of other expressions which are put into different words in texts or questions, and elicit likely alternative ways of expressing them. For example:

eventually   cost of a ticket   bad weather   by herself
affected   seasons   male   job   have to   fix   won
these days   buses and trains   amateur

5.12 Predicting from introductions

LEVEL	**Elementary and above**
AIMS	**To predict number of speakers, vocabulary areas, verb tenses, and functions in listening comprehension texts**
TIME	**30–60 minutes**
PREPARATION	None.

PROCEDURE

1 Focus attention on the introduction to a listening comprehension task. If the introduction is not on the question paper but on the recording, write it up on the board or OHP.

2 Ask the class what they expect to hear in terms of the number of speakers, vocabulary areas, verb tenses, functions, and (with more advanced students) register. You may also want to ask about accents, speed, and relationships between speakers.

3 Play the tape once so that students can check their predictions.

4 In groups, the students study more introductions and list the features they expect will be in the recordings.

5 The students listen again and check.

6 Groups think of as many likely exam listening comprehension topics as they can, or, if they are not yet familiar enough with the exam, they choose topics from their coursebook. They write an introduction and predict the language content in each case.

Example

Look at this introduction to a listening comprehension test and note down what you expect to hear.

'You will hear a radio weather forecast.'

Number of speakers: *one*

Vocabulary areas: *kinds of weather, figures, time expressions*

Verb tenses: *future forms, modals*

Functions: *predicting, speculating*

Now do the same with these:

'You will hear a recorded message at a tourist information office.'

'You will hear an extract from an interview with a rock star.'

'You will hear someone explaining how to get to a city centre pub.'

'You will hear a teacher and a director of studies arguing.'

'You will hear an extract from a speech by a politician.'

'You will hear part of a review of a controversial new movie.'

'You will hear a conversation between a doctor and her patient.'

'You will hear several phone-in complaints about a TV show.'

'You will hear an oral examiner talking about candidates.'

5.13 Inferring from conversations

LEVEL

Upper-intermediate and above

AIMS

To develop the skill of inferring information in short listening comprehension conversations; to provide speaking practice by role-playing test dialogues

TIME

Variable

PREPARATION

1 You will need some exam tasks which test comprehension of dialogues.

2 Put a list of possible exam listening comprehension conversation situations on a worksheet, the board, or OHP.

PROCEDURE

1 Focus on a model dialogue and elicit questions about it. Then ask students to think of more questions like those in the box below. Get the class to note them down.

Possible questions about a dialogue

Where is this happening?
What is the relationship between the speakers?
What are they doing?
What kind of people are they?
What are their jobs?
What might have happened before the conversation?
What is the main point of the conversation?
What might happen after the conversation?
Is the first speaker asking a question or making a statement?
With what kind of sentence does the second speaker respond?
What is the first speaker's attitude during the conversation?
How might their attitudes change as a result of the conversation?

Photocopiable © Oxford University Press

2 As a class, students listen to a number of the dialogues, answering as many as possible of the questions about each.

3 Students do the exam task. Check their answers.

4 Choosing one of the situations from the list, students ask questions about it and use the answers to decide how the dialogue should be spoken.

5 Two of the group act out the dialogue, a third plays the role of narrator and asks an inferential question such as 'What will the man probably do?', which the fourth answers in his or her own words.

6 Students repeat this with other situations, taking turns at different roles.

Example

> After you hear a question, read the four possible answers in your test book and choose the best answer.
>
> **On the recording, you will hear:**
>
> **(man)**   I should have plenty of time tomorrow—I'll finish the report in the morning.
>
> **(woman)**   I'm sorry but I want you to start on another project then.
>
> **(narrator)** What does the woman imply?
>
> **In your text book, you will read:**
>
> (A) He should finish the report tomorrow.
> (B) He should finish the report today.
> (C) He can finish the report today or tomorrow.
> (D) He should start on the project today.

(TOEFL, Section 1: Listening Comprehension)

VARIATION

More advanced classes can design their own multiple-choice questions at stage 5: the examinee temporarily leaves the group while the speakers and narrator confer. They write down the four options, as in a test paper, and tell the examinee to choose the best one.

5.14 Recognizing the main points

LEVEL

Lower-intermediate and above

AIMS

To practise listening for the main points of a longer listening comprehension text; to role-play the speakers

TIME

40 minutes

PREPARATION

1 Listen to (or read a transcript of) a dialogue and make a list of the main points in your own words.

2 Put these points in jumbled order on the board or OHP.

PROCEDURE

1 Make sure everyone understands the list of points you have written up.

2 Play the tape. As they listen students put the points in the right order. Check their answers.

3 Put the class into pairs and tell student A to listen to the first speaker and student B to listen to the second speaker. While they listen they are to make notes on the situation, 'their' speaker, and the relationship between the two speakers. Play the tape once, leaving out any exam instructions for the moment.

4 Using the list of points from stage 2 and their notes from stage 3, students recreate the dialogue by role-playing 'their' speakers.

5 Students listen to the tape again—this time with the exam instructions—and do the exam task, at the same time comparing the dialogue with their own conversation. Play the recording a fourth time if necessary.

Example

'Excuse me, I work for the City Council. Would you have time to answer a few questions about the proposed new concert hall?'

'Concert hall?'

'Yes, have you heard about the City Council's plans?'

'Oh, I think I did. Well, my bus won't be here for a while.'

'Great. Well first of all, could I have a few details for our records? 'Obviously, you live around here...'

'Yeah.'

'And you're, sorry, I have to ask, um, are you eighteen or younger?'

'Oh, I don't mind. I was twenty only two days ago.'

'Well, belated happy birthday! And what's your occupation?'

'I'm in my second year at the technical college.'

'And do you like music, going to concerts, that sort of thing? Do you go to them often?'

'Well, I go out three or four evenings a week, but usually I go to the cinema or disco.'

(*Cambridge First Certificate in English, transcript extract*)

Main points: how old she is
where she goes in her free time
where she lives
if she is in a hurry
what she does
if she knows about the council's plans

Situation: two people at a bus stop
Speaker A: interviewer, enthusiastic
Speaker B: person-in-the-street, cautious at first
Relationship: strangers

VARIATION 1

With more advanced classes, add one or two false events to the list. Students then also have to choose which ones to include.

VARIATION 2

This activity can also be used with reading comprehension texts.

COMMENTS

Explain to the class that it is easier to understand a recorded dialogue if they can picture the speakers as real people in a situation they can imagine.

5.15 Predicting the answers

LEVEL   **Lower-intermediate and above**

AIMS   **To predict text content in interviews; to practise interviews by role-playing text speakers**

TIME   **30 minutes**

PREPARATION   Choose a comprehension interview which deals with a topical issue likely to be of interest to your students. Ignore the exam task.

PROCEDURE   1 Play the tape, leaving out any exam task instructions but including the introduction. Pause after each of the interviewer's questions to enable the class to note it down. Replay or dictate the question if necessary.

2 Elicit likely responses to the question and then play the tape so that the class can compare their ideas with what the interviewee says.

3 Pair the class in the roles of interviewer and interviewee. Tell them to relate questions and answers on the same issue to their own country.

Example

'Neighbours'

Jameson: A survey in this week's *Sunday Times* showed that one million householders in the UK would like to move because of the people next door. Not everybody knows but it is the Environmental Health Officer's job to deal with problems like these. This morning, we have in the studio John Salmon, the Chief Environmental Health Officer for Barnet in North London. John, other Europeans, the Spanish, the Italians, the Germans, do they dislike their neighbours as intensely as we seem to?

Salmon: _____

Jameson: What's the most common problem then?

Salmon: _____

Jameson: Noise complaints are on the increase, aren't they?

Salmon: _____

(*Cambridge Certificate in Advanced English, extract*)

VARIATION   If you can obtain a recording of an exam interview (see Bibliography, page 164), or record a mock interview of a student, get the class to predict the candidate's answers and then role-play the situation as above.

5.16 Who said what?

<u>LEVEL</u>   **Elementary and above**

<u>AIM</u>   **To introduce students to multiple matching (listening for detail and specific information)**

<u>TIME</u>   **25 minutes**

<u>PREPARATION</u>   **1** Choose a suitable multiple matching task similar to those in the examples below.

2 Listen to the tape. For each question, note down an expression from the recording which gives a clue to the correct answer. With lower-level classes you may want to give more than one clue per question.

<u>PROCEDURE</u>   **1** On a piece of paper, each student draws a column with numbered spaces for their answers.

2 The students do the exam task in the usual way, listening once or twice according to the exam format and filling in the answers. Do not correct them at this stage.

3 Put the clues on the board or OHP, numbered according to the answers they relate to.

4 Tell the students to draw a second, similar answer column alongside the first.

5 They listen to the recording again, using the clues to decide whether or not to change their answers. They write their final choices in the second column, without erasing the answers in the first column.

6 Collect in the answer papers and go through the answers with the class, eliciting and/or explaining the relevance of the clues. (See answer key at end of chapter.)

Example

You will hear five different men talking about journeys they have made.
For Questions 19–23, choose from the list A–F what happened to each one on his journey. Use the letters only once. There is one extra letter which you do not need to use.

A He realised he had forgotten something.	Speaker 1		19		19
B He met someone he knew.	Speaker 2		20		20
C He saw some beautiful scenery.	Speaker 3		21		21
D He was involved in an accident.	Speaker 4		22		22
E He arrived late at his destination.	Speaker 5		23		23
F He got lost on the way.					

Clues

19 – *I didn't have a clue where I was*
20 – *I kept them waiting*

21 – *then I remembered that I'd left it at Judy's place*
22 – *I had to hear the same old rubbish I always get from him*
23 – *then there was this bump*

Tapescript

SPEAKER 1 So there I was, coming into the place, and I couldn't see any signs. I thought it would be best to stop and ask someone before I took a wrong turning. So I wound down the window and asked this passer-by. He was very friendly and he patiently explained everything. Well I thanked him and set off again, and a few minutes later I was stuck in a load of traffic somewhere in the countryside and I didn't have a clue where I was. He must have got it wrong, because I'd done just what he said. Anyway, I just pulled over and stopped the engine and thought 'What do I do now?' It was just as well I'd left early enough or I'd never have got there on time.

PAUSE 2 seconds

SPEAKER 2 Well, I rushed along the platform and got on just before it left and I breathed a sigh of relief, I can tell you, 'cause I'd been sure I was going to miss it and the people who were meeting me at the other end would have to wait. Anyway, I settled into my seat and I was just staring out of the window and watching the world go by when suddenly the thing ground to a halt. And then there was this announcement, that due to some problem or other with the electrics, we were going to be stuck there for quite some time. So I ended up having to get off, change and go by a different route, which meant that I kept them waiting anyway!

PAUSE 2 seconds

SPEAKER 3 Well, I'd been going for so long that I was virtually falling off the bike, so I pulled into the side for a sit-down. And there I was, in the middle of nowhere, and there was nobody around—except for the occasional fellow cyclist who I waved to—and all you could see was miles and miles of the most incredibly dull, flat landscape. Anyway, I thought, 'What's the name of that hotel I'm staying in tonight?' So I looked in my bag for all that stuff and then I remembered I'd left it at Judy's place. So there I was, with nowhere to go. Well, I went into the town anyway and some kind person pointed me at a place and I stayed there.

PAUSE 2 seconds

SPEAKER 4 Well I got there really early like they tell you to, so I had to do loads of sitting around until we were called. And then eventually we *were*, and we all filed onto the plane, and that's when I started to get really excited, because I was finally off and in just a few hours I'd be in one of the most wonderful places in the world. Anyway, then I was looking for my seat—there was some mix-up because I couldn't find my boarding card at first—and then, would you believe it, I bumped into *him*! He was in the next seat to mine! So instead of a nice, relaxing flight, I had to hear all the same old rubbish I always get from him!

PAUSE 2 seconds

SPEAKER 5 Well, I was just looking out of the window and everything was going smoothly and I was just thinking 'I can't remember when I last took a trip like this'. And I was thinking how bare the landscape was. I fetched the map book out of my bag out of curiosity but I couldn't work out where we were at all. Anyway, then there was this bump—I didn't see what happened, I was at the back. All I saw was the driver arguing with someone in a car—they were really screaming at each other. Well, there was a lengthy delay but eventually we got going and we must have gone faster after that because we still got there on time.

(*Cambridge First Certificate in English*, Revised 1996)

FOLLOW-UP

Study the differences between the answers in the two columns. A significant improvement in the second column would indicate that the clues have been useful. This should be pointed out to the class and the activity repeated with other materials. On this and subsequent occasions some or all of the clues can be elicited at stage 3.

VARIATION 1

With lower levels, pause after the class have heard the recording once (step 2) and ask the class to identify each speaker's situation. In the text above, for example, they are: (1) car (2) train   (3) bicycle   (4) aeroplane   (5) bus.

VARIATION 2

This technique can also be used with similar task-types involving conversations.

Question paper (extract)

> You will hear a conversation which takes place in a hotel, between a tour guide and some people who are staying there, Mrs Walsh and her son, Paul.
>
> Answer Questions 24–30 by writing T (for tour guide),
>   W (for Mrs Walsh), or P (for Paul) in the boxes provided.
>
> 24 Who is cheerful at first?   24

Tapescript (extract)

Guide	... seems to be fine. I'm sure they'll all enjoy – hello Mrs Walsh, how are you today? Ready for the trip this afternoon?
Mrs Walsh	I have a serious problem. Paul will bear me out.
Guide	Hello, Paul, how's it going?
Paul	Um, hi.
Guide	So, what can I do for you? More sunshine?

(*Cambridge First Certificate in English,* Revised 1996)

Clues: 24 – *fine, enjoy, sunshine.*

COMMENTS

Also point out the importance of concentrating on *how* the words are spoken, so that the speakers' feelings and intentions are fully appreciated.

Answers

5.16   19 F   20 E   21 A   22 B   23 D   24 T

6 Speaking

The activities in this chapter should greatly help students prepare for examination papers such as 'Speaking', 'Interview', 'Oral', 'Oral Examination', 'Oral Assessment', 'Oral Interview', 'Oral Interaction', and 'Test of Spoken English'.

At lower levels candidates are usually expected to be able to talk about themselves and other topics. They will need to demonstrate pronunciation that is intelligible, sufficient accuracy in grammar and vocabulary to communicate, language that is in general appropriate to the function, and the ability to participate in conversations. At higher levels they may have to show, for example, their ability to negotiate and collaborate, plus interactional, social, and transactional skills (Cambridge CAE), or the ability to communicate successfully in academic or professional environments (TOEFL TSE). Assessment criteria may include grammar, vocabulary, pronunciation, and interactive communication (Cambridge FCE); fluency and intelligibility, grammar and vocabulary, comprehension, and sociolinguistic proficiency (MELAB); and readiness, usage, pronunciation, and focus (Trinity).

Most boards use an oral interview, although in the TSE and the Oxford-Arels exams candidates listen to a tape and have their responses recorded. Trinity, Cambridge CCSE, and EAL conduct the exams at the centre where the learners are studying—individually in the case of Trinity, individually or with another candidate in CCSE, in small groups in EAL. Many exam interviews are done in pairs, with the speaking focus shifting between examiner and candidate or candidate and candidate. Examiners have noted that students who are accustomed to working with partners tend to be better prepared for this format, so plenty of pair-work practice is provided in this and other chapters of this book. All of the activities can be used to practise the examiner–candidate focus of exams such as Cambridge CPE, MELAB, and the IB, and in most cases are suitable for—or can be adapted to—the candidate–candidate format used in Cambridge FCE and CAE.

For exams such as Cambridge CCSE and PET, successful task completion depends on using a range of language functions. There are activities in this chapter, therefore, which help develop the ability to describe (6.3, 6.4, 6.5, 6.6), focus on expressing emotions and opinions (6.9), and practise giving instructions (6.14). Most of the activities are suitable for students taking any of the exams listed on pages 159–63, particularly those involving an oral interview. Activity 6.1 (see also 1.2) focuses on the different stages of the kind of interview used in most of the Cambridge exams, while 6.13 and 6.14 are especially useful for rehearsing the complete interview procedure. Others concentrate on stages of the PET, FCE, CAE, and CPE oral such as socializing and giving personal information (6.2), discussing pictures (6.3, 6.4, 6.5), or interactive tasks in which the candidates talk to each other (6.1, 6.7). For suggestions on talking about set books (CPE), see 3.15 and 6.7.

All the most common types of task are covered, from giving a prepared talk in 6.10 (CPE, IELTS, TSE, Trinity, IB, EAL) to social situations in 6.11 (Oxford-Arels, ICC 1 and 2) and taking part in role-plays and simulations (UCLES, Oxford-Arels, ICC, IOL, EAL) in 6.8 and 6.12. See also 1.8 for discussing and inferring from texts in oral exams (CPE, IB), and reading aloud (Oxford-Arels, EAL) in 4.5.

Where the oral takes the form of recorded questions, it is advisable to choose activities which relate to specific components of the exam in question, for example 6.9 for the TSE and 6.11 for the Oxford-Arels. Activities 6.3, 6.4, 6.5, and 6.10 are also recommended for taped orals.

Quite apart from all the possible ways of preparing for the oral exam (for some suggestions, see 1.2), the exam classroom provides a wide range of opportunities for students to practise speaking. Working in pairs, groups, or as a class, there is enormous scope for exchanging opinions and making suggestions on the work students have done or are about to do, the materials they are using, and the exam itself. This forms an essential part of many of the activities in this book, and can change an exam lesson from a disjointed and fragmented mixture of exercises into a smoothly linked progression from one stage to another.

6.1 Interview questions

LEVEL	**Intermediate and above**
AIMS	**To increase awareness of interview format and exam questions; to practise interactive tasks with other candidates**
TIME	**45 minutes**
PREPARATION	1 Make a list of likely interview questions and instructions for the exam your students are taking, possibly using a recording of a transcript of an actual exam. For example: *Please talk to each other and decide which would be the best solution.*

Make sure there are some questions from all stages of the interview.

2 Split each sentence into two parts and jumble the second halves. Make a worksheet or OHP transparency.

Example Worksheet

Form complete sentences by matching A–L with 1–12:

1	I'd like you to compare these	A	the best to the worst.
2	How do you like	B	when you leave school?
3	What's your opinion	C	would be the easiest.
4	What do you feel about	D	two diagrams.
5	Which of the three stages	E	and you are the policeman.
6	What do you think is	F	to spend your free time?
7	How long have you	G	of films like that?
8	Imagine you are the driver	H	that thing in the background?
9	Put these in order, from	I	in the picture?
10	Decide which method	J	would you do first; which last?
11	What do you want to do	K	been learning English?
12	What can you see	L	oil companies dumping rigs?

At which stage (a–d) of the interview would each of these be asked?

Photocopiable © Oxford University Press

PROCEDURE

1 Hand out the worksheet or focus attention on the OHP. Students match the sentence halves and check with their partners.

2 List the stages of the interview on the board, for example:

a giving personal information and socializing;
b talking about photos, individually;
c a task with another candidate, such as comparing, decision-making, ordering, prioritizing, or role-playing;
d exchanging opinions with another candidate and/or the examiner.

3 Pairs match each of the completed sentences with the most likely stage of the interview.

4 Where there are a number of possible task types at one of the stages a–d, ask the class which sentence would go with each task. For example at stage (c):

1/D   comparing
5/J   prioritizing
8/E   role-playing
9/A   ordering
10/C   decision-making

5 Choose one of these task types and elicit other instructions and questions that could be used by the examiner. Put them on the board.

6 Using materials similar to those in the exam for this task, students interview each other.

7 When they have finished, ask the class what new words and phrases they have heard during the course of the activity.

FOLLOW-UP Repeat Procedure stages 5–7 with other task types from stage 4.

COMMENTS Make sure the class realize that in many of the most popular modern exams the interview has a number of clearly defined stages, often with shifts in focus such as from examiner–candidate to candidate–candidate.

There is an answer key for the example exercise at the end of the chapter.

6.2 Talking about yourself

LEVEL Elementary and above

AIMS To practise breaking the interview ice; to heighten awareness of likely interview questions

TIME 45 minutes

PREPARATION Draw up a list of the kinds of questions that come up at the start of the oral exam, possibly from the teacher's (or self-study) edition of a book of exam practice tests.

PROCEDURE 1 With low-level classes put your questions on the board or OHP. With higher levels, elicit as many questions as possible or get groups to brainstorm them, adding questions from your list if necessary.

2 Focus attention on somebody in a picture in the students' coursebook or exam practice book. The class imagine this person is a candidate and invent personal details for him or her. These might include name, nationality, home town, job or studies, hobbies, reasons for learning English, and plans for the future. This could be done in pairs or groups. The whole class then share their information and decide on a 'definitive version'.

3 You take the part of the candidate and answer questions from the class, using the details invented by them.

4 In pairs, students choose another picture of a person from their coursebooks. Student A is the 'candidate' and spends a couple of minutes thinking up imaginary personal details. Student B is the 'examiner' and asks the questions. Then they swap roles so that student A can ask questions.

5 When they have finished, ask the class what questions they asked and put any new ones on the board.

6 Students change partners and interview each other, this time talking about themselves.

VARIATION

1 Find photos of five people who are about the same age range and background as your students, if possible in working, social, or sporting contexts that reflect their personalities and interests. Photocopy them onto a worksheet and make a copy for each group.

2 On separate pieces of paper write brief first-person self-descriptions for the five people, including 'How old I am, Where I live, What I do, My hobbies, Why I'm learning English, My plans for the future'. Make a copy for each group.

3 In groups students match the photos and the text. Check their answers and follow up by asking them to suggest more information about each person.

COMMENTS

Explain to the class that this activity will help prepare them for the first few minutes of their exam interview, when it is vital that they are able to settle and begin to show their ability as quickly as possible.

6.3 Pictures: questions and answers

LEVEL

Elementary and above

AIMS

To practise asking and answering questions about a picture; to raise awareness of picture and question types

TIME

50 minutes

PREPARATION

1 Ensure students have access to plenty of the kinds of pictures used in the oral exam. These might be from past papers, in practice tests, or on worksheets you have prepared.

2 Select a typical exam picture, perhaps showing people involved in some kind of activity, with plenty of detail in the background. Make a list of possible questions about the setting, the subject, and the activity. With more advanced students ask what might have led up to the situation shown, what could happen next and 'What if . . .?' questions.

PROCEDURE

1 In groups students decide which types of photo are used most often in the exams, for example how many feature people, animals, or objects. Students also make a note of the most common scenes and activities such as the weather, everyday street events, topical issues, sports and hobbies, work, entertainment, education, food and drink, family life, health and welfare, holidays and travel, institutions, and relationships. Then they report back to the class.

2 Students look at the picture you have chosen. Elicit questions about it and put them on the board. Add your own and tell the class to copy all of them down for future reference.

3 Elicit the answers. Put the good ones on the board and ask the class why they are good (they give the kind of information required in the exam).

4 Students in pairs choose a picture. They practise asking and answering questions about it. This can be repeated with other pictures.

FOLLOW-UP

Ask the class which questions were difficult to answer, and why. Elicit and suggest strategies for dealing with these questions, such as paraphrasing if they don't know a word, asking the examiner to repeat the question, or asking for clarification.

VARIATION

For lower-intermediate levels and above.
Put students into two teams. Give both teams the same picture and tell them they have ten minutes to draw up a list of questions. Then a member of team A asks team B a question. Team B gets two points for a really good answer; one point for an adequate one; no points if the answer is wrong or if they take too long to answer. Then team B asks team A a question, and so on until neither side has more questions to ask. The team with the most points wins.

6.4 Pictures: what and where?

LEVEL

Elementary and above

AIMS

To practise describing pictures using prepositions of place; to build vocabulary

TIME

30 minutes

PREPARATION

Choose two different pictures, possibly from the students' coursebook. Each should contain a similarly large number of objects, some of which have names that will be new to many of the students.

PROCEDURE

1 Put the class into two teams. Explain that in round 1 each team must look at a picture and remember as many objects as they can.

2 Tell team A which picture they are to look at and let them study it for three minutes. They can confer.

3 They cover up the picture and each student in turn tells the class the name of an object they have seen. Give them one point for each object correctly named (in English), keeping a record of the score.

4 Repeat the procedure with team B.

5 In round 2, students look again at their pictures, but this time they must remember where each object is in relation to another.

6 When they have covered up their pictures again, students get one point for each correct sentence along the lines of 'There's a video behind the poster', and so on.

7 The team with the most points wins.

8 As a class, look once more at the pictures. Elicit the names of any objects which have not been mentioned, as well as their positions in relation to other things.

Example

'There's a personal stereo next to the CD player.'
'In the case there's a pair of earrings.'
'There are some cards on top of the box.'

VARIATION

Practise expressions which describe position in the picture rather than in relation to other objects, such as:

'In the background there's an advertisement.'
'There are some cassettes on the left-hand side.'
'At the top of the picture there seems to be some writing.'

6.5 Identifying from descriptions

LEVEL

Intermediate and above

AIMS

To practice comparing and contrasting using visual prompts; to develop intensive listening skills

TIME

60 minutes +

PREPARATION

Find photos containing a variety of people, objects, or places. For best results they should not be too dissimilar from each other, for example people at a sports or cultural event, cars in the street, or buildings in a particular city.

PROCEDURE

1 Present or revise language such as descriptive adjectives, collocations (*fair hair, heavy rain,* etc.), comparative forms, conjunctions (*but, while, though, whereas*).

2 Ensure everyone is looking at the same photo(s). Without saying which you have chosen, compare and contrast a person, thing, or place with others. For example:

He looks about the same age as the rest of the men in the group of people on the far left. He's a bit shorter than most of the others and perhaps not quite so slim as some of them, although he's certainly not as overweight as that one with the hat on. He's wearing a jacket that's darker than anyone else's. He's got longish hair compared to the others and he's the only one who's got a moustache.

The class must try and guess who or what you are talking about. Start with general observations and use language just a little above the level the class are used to, pausing regularly for them to absorb the information and, possibly, tell you the answer. Gradually make the clues more specific and the language easier—or slower—until someone has identified the subject correctly. Repeat using other people or items from the same photo(s).

3 Show the class more photos and elicit sentences that compare and contrast features of them.

4 Put the class into groups and give them pictures of, for example, famous people, regions of their country, or popular hobbies. Students decide on a picture, make notes on how their choice differs from others and then a spokesperson tells you about the subject. This time you have to guess the answers. This also provides an opportunity for you to check for and correct any serious language errors before students go off to work on their own.

5 In pairs, one student describes/contrasts/compares the contents of a picture in the coursebook while the other identifies. Then they swap roles. Lower levels could discuss, for example, the difference in colour, size, shape, price, and taste of fruit or vegetables; higher levels could imagine a hypothetical change to the subject and compare or contrast with the reality, for example: *If she could train full-time she would be able to run two seconds faster.*

<table>
<tr><td>VARIATION 1</td><td>At stage 2, also say what is different about someone, something or somewhere well known to the class, for example:
It is a city with more ancient buildings than almost anywhere else in the country, and has a bigger university than the capital, although of course it isn't quite as internationally famous and it doesn't have the same number of visitors as …</td></tr>
<tr><td>VARIATION 2</td><td>After stage 4, divide the class into two teams. The first team to call out the right answer gets 2 points. If team A makes an incorrect identification they lose a point and the question is offered to team B, who receive one point if they get the answer right. After a number of descriptions, the team with the most points wins.</td></tr>
</table>

6.6 Communication strategies

<table>
<tr><td>LEVEL</td><td>Intermediate and above</td></tr>
<tr><td>AIMS</td><td>To identify and use communication strategies in oral exams; to practise describing</td></tr>
<tr><td>TIME</td><td>40 minutes</td></tr>
<tr><td>PREPARATION</td><td>

1 Either record a mock interview with a strong student or obtain a pre-recorded sample interview with a successful candidate.

2 Identify the communication strategies used by the candidate. These could include paraphrasing: *it's where you buy stamps* for 'post office'; asking for clarification: *do you mean the one on the left?*; self-correcting: *what I mean is*; approximating: *or that kind of thing*; countering interruption: *if I could just finish this point* and even—as long as it is not overdone—hesitating: saying *Well let me see …* while collecting one's thoughts is better than total silence. Make a list of the strategies and give each a reference letter.

3 On a transcript of the relevant part of the dialogue, underline or highlight the words or phrases used to express the communication strategies and number them. There may be more than one example of each strategy.

</td></tr>
</table>

PROCEDURE

1 Without looking at the transcripts, the class listen to the recording and answer some simple gist questions on the topic of the interview.

2 Play the recording again, this time eliciting comments on the candidate's performance in terms of fluency, pronunciation, grammar, vocabulary, and ability to communicate.

3 Students study the transcripts and comment on language errors.

4 They match the underlined expressions with the list of strategies. (See key at end of chapter.)

5 In each case, elicit other expressions to achieve the same communicative aim. Write them on the board or OHP.

6 Ask the class questions which make them use communication strategies. For example, point at objects with difficult names— such as *coat-hanger*, *board-cleaner* or *pencil-sharpener*—and ask what they are (paraphrasing). Ask questions that require clarification: *Where's the best shop?*, *At what time do people eat?*, *How many of you live here?*, or an approximate answer: *What's the population of Asia, How far away is the nearest star?* Put some of the expressions they use on the board and add more, for example: *It's the thing you use for ...*, *What kind of ... do you mean? It must be about ...*

7 Using materials similar to those in the interview they have heard, students ask each other questions in pairs.

Example

> *Which of the strategies a–e is used in 1–5 below?*
> **a** approximating   **b** asking for clarification
> **c** self-correcting   **d** hesitation   **e** paraphrasing
> (*The candidate is shown a photograph.*)
>
> Irini: There are four boys that they're sitting on a table (1) . . . I mean on some chairs. They're in a library, perhaps in a school library. Two of them are writing and two others are looking some books.
>
> Interviewer: Could you describe the boy on the left?
>
> Irini: On the left. All right. (2) He's the one who's writing something isn't he?
>
> Interviewer: Yes.
>
> Irini: OK. He has (3) er blond er hair, we can say quite long with (4) a bit down to his eyes. He's wearing a black sweater, he's writing, or copying, something, and he's really very concentrated to what he's doing.
>
> Interviewer: How old is he about, do you think?
>
> Irini: Well . . . seventeen, sixteen – (5) something like that.

VARIATION	More advanced students find the expressions in the transcript for themselves.
COMMENTS	Point out that competent speakers often manage to communicate well by using virtually the same techniques in English as those they use in their first language. The words are different but the strategies are similar—and the candidate's confidence is greatly increased.

6.7 Interview interaction

LEVEL	**Elementary and above**
AIMS	**To simulate examiner–candidate and candidate–candidate interaction; to practise writing questions and answers**
TIME	**45 minutes**
PREPARATION	Choose three oral exam tasks which use texts or diagrams. Select one as an example and note down some likely questions and answers about the material. The questions could be the kind an examiner or another candidate might ask, depending on the exam format.
PROCEDURE	1 Show students the task and write up the answers—but not the questions—on the board, the OHP, or a worksheet.

Example

You are making plans over the phone to go to Ireland. Discuss the information in this leaflet with your friend.

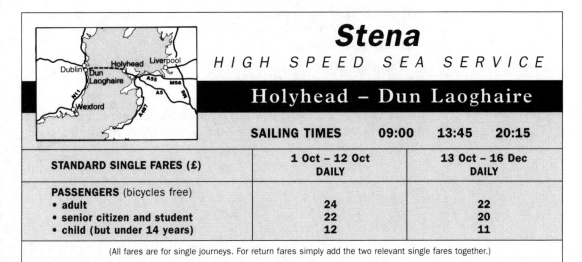

Stena

HIGH SPEED SEA SERVICE

Holyhead – Dun Laoghaire

| SAILING TIMES | | 09:00 | 13:45 | 20:15 |

STANDARD SINGLE FARES (£)	1 Oct – 12 Oct DAILY	13 Oct – 16 Dec DAILY
PASSENGERS (bicycles free)		
• adult	24	22
• senior citizen and student	22	20
• child (but under 14 years)	12	11

(All fares are for single journeys. For return fares simply add the two relevant single fares together.)

1	*How long does it take*?	'About an hour and a half, I think.'
2	_____?	'From Holyhead in North Wales.'
3	_____?	'Dun Laoghaire, near Dublin.'
4	_____?	'It depends. It'd be cheaper if we go on the 13th.'
5	_____?	'Well, for two it would be £40 one-way.'
6	_____?	'Then it'd be eighty.'
7	_____?	'Well, the first one's at nine in the morning.'
8	_____?	'By getting a very early train, I guess!'
9	_____?	'Thirty minutes before departure, it says.'
10	_____?	'Yes, I think we should.'

2 Working individually, students practise writing questions using the answers as prompts.

3 Discuss the questions as a class. Elicit the types of question which tend to be asked in this kind of conversation: often *Who/What/Where/When/How*? about the basic facts, followed by questions about variations, hypothetical situations, and the other person's opinion. With less advanced students, put the basic question forms on the board or OHP.

4 In groups of at least three, students look at another similar task. In each group, student A writes questions about the material and—without letting the rest of the group see them—passes them to student B.

5 Student B answers each question aloud and the rest of the group must say what the question was. Student A says whether they are right or not.

6 Using the same material or that of a similar task, the group take it in turn to be A, B, or 'listeners'.

VARIATION

Instead of writing the questions, student A whispers them to student B, who then answers aloud. The activity continues as above.

6.8 Role-plays and simulations

LEVEL

Elementary and above

AIMS

To familiarize students with task types by writing prompts and functional exponents, and then taking part in the role-plays and/or simulations they have designed

TIME

45 minutes

PREPARATION

Prepare a list of enough role-play or simulation situations for there to be one for each group in the class.

PROCEDURE

1 As a class, look at some examples of role-plays or simulations in the coursebook or exam practice material. Ask the class what sort of things are written on the prompt cards (for simulations) or role-cards.

2 Give each group of students a situation and tell them to write a prompt card or role-card.

Example

SIMULATION – organizing a party

Your group has decided to have a party. Discuss and decide:
- whose house it will be at;
- how many people can come;
- what time it will start and finish;
- what music there will be;
- which day it will be;
- who you will invite;
- what there will be to drink and eat;
- what to do about the neighbours.

ROLE-PLAY – salesperson/customer

Student A
You are a door-to-door salesperson. You are sure that what you are selling is very good, but today nobody has bought anything. You are making your last call. You must sell something or you will lose your job!

Student B
You are a student. You are working hard at home. Somebody knocks at the door and tries to sell you something. You are not very interested and you don't have much money.

Photocopiable © Oxford University Press

With younger and/or less advanced students you may wish to be on hand with ideas.

3 Students write a list of useful expressions for the situation or roles. For the simulation above, for example:

How about ...?   Why don't we ...?
What if we ...?   Do you think we should ...?
I think we'd better ...   I'd rather ...

They could also suggest vocabulary, such as *guests*, *host*, *snacks*, *loud*, *chat*, *dance*, *complain*.

4 Students exchange cards and lists with another group and do the simulation or the role-play.

5 Students tell the group that designed the task how it went, whether any improvements could be made, and what other useful expressions were used.

VARIATION

At stage 4, one student from each group moves to the group doing the task written by his or her group. After the group has done the task, this student reports back to his or her group.

6.9 Saying what you think

LEVEL

Intermediate and above

AIMS

To practise asking for, expressing, and justifying opinions

TIME

30–45 minutes

PREPARATION

Prepare two 60-second talks on topics that you feel quite strongly about, for example in answer to questions such as 'Do you think teachers are paid enough?'. Include expressions like those in stage 5 below.

PROCEDURE

1 Speak to the class about the subject without mentioning the topic by name. The class have to guess what the question might be.

2 Choose another subject and do the same again. This time, as well as guessing the topic, the class note down any expressions they hear you say that they might want to use to express their own opinions.

3 In groups, students list topics which arouse strong feelings, for example: equal opportunities, conscription, animal welfare, a shorter working week, bureaucrats, advertising, traffic wardens, junk food, lone parents, politicians, bad drivers, TV quiz shows, prison sentences, millionaire rock singers, bosses, public transport, tourists, censorship, multinationals, noisy neighbours, shopping in the sales. Topics for younger students might include: adults, troublesome brothers/sisters, pocket money, minimum-age limits, school rules, school uniforms, homework ... and teachers!

4 Each group in turn asks you a question in a form similar to that used in the exam. For example:

> 'Some people say that we need to build more roads. Others believe that more roads just lead to more traffic. We'd like to know what you think about this issue.'
>
> *(TOEFL, Test of Spoken English)*

5 After a few seconds' thought, speak for about one minute. If you can avoid making your answer sound contrived, sprinkle it with more expressions like these (or put some of them on the board):

In my opinion, ...	Personally, I think ...
I'm convinced that ...	I reckon ...
It seems to me ...	To my mind ...
To tell the truth ...	My own feeling is ...
As I see it, ...	The thing that ... me is ...
I really believe that ...	As far as I'm concerned ...
What I mean is ...	Why not look at it this way ...
Let me put it another way ...	The point I'm trying to make is ...
It may seem a bit, ... but ...	There's no need to worry about that, ...

6 In pairs, students choose more topics to talk about. Their partners listen and try to guess the questions—as they did with you at stage 1. Encourage them to include expressions from your answers.

VARIATION

Instead of speaking to the class, you may prefer to use an extract from a pre-recorded audio or video tape, or a tape of yourself speaking. Play the recording once right through, then rewind and focus on the key expressions.

COMMENTS

This activity also provides an opportunity to practise the communication strategies in 6.6.

6.10 Giving a prepared talk

LEVEL   **Intermediate and above**

AIMS   **To practise giving a talk in the oral exam**

TIME   **30–40 minutes**

PREPARATION   Make a list of four topics which could come up as the subject of the prepared talk in the exam, for example: *What makes a good film, How to learn my language, A dangerous situation,* and *Living in another country.*

PROCEDURE   1 On the board or OHP, write the topics and underneath put a list of possible headings for each. If it is a conflict in the news, for instance, the main points could be:

a) Where is it taking place   d) The rights and wrongs
b) Who is involved   e) Similar events elsewhere
c) Why it is happening   f) Predictions and solutions

For a more personal topic such as *My favourite sport,* suitable prompts might be:

a) Why I first took an interest   d) Why I enjoy it
   in it
b) Any special equipment   e) Any limitations and how I
   needed   deal with them
c) The rules; where and how   f) My future plans
   it is played

2 Put the class into groups of four. Each student chooses one of the topics and makes notes under the appropriate headings.

3 Feed in relevant functional language. If the topic is *My hobby,* for example, this could be sequencing and expressing likes/preferences: *The first thing you do is … then …; What I like best about it is …; I'd much rather … than …*

4 Each student gives his or her talk to the other members of the group. To help build the speaker's confidence, encourage the listeners to give non-verbal signs of interest such as nodding and smiling where appropriate.

5 When the speaker has finished, the other students ask questions about the topic and keep a note of the points they raise.

6 The other students give the speaker a list of these extra points in case he or she needs to give a similar talk in the future.

COMMENT   At stage 4, you may want to record the talk for analysis and feedback purposes.

6.11 What would you say?

LEVEL Upper-intermediate and above

AIMS To practise responding in social situations

TIME 40 minutes

PREPARATION 1 Find a list of situations in the coursebook, or make your own list on a worksheet.

2 On a second worksheet put a list of responses to situations—not those from stage 1—and cut it up so that there are four responses for each group of four students.

PROCEDURE 1 Read out a few of the situations from the first worksheet and elicit the responses. Correct where necessary and suggest other possible responses.

Example

> Now you'll hear nine situations in which you might find yourself. Say what it seems natural to say in each situation. Ready?
>
> 7 *You're on a train and have been talking to a lady in your compartment. When you reach your destination and are about to get off the train, what do you say to her?*
>
> (EIGHT SECONDS)
>
> 8 *You're having a coffee break with a colleague. He's telling you all about a problem he's having, but you have an appointment with a client in ten minutes. What do you say?*
>
> (SEVEN SECONDS)
>
> 9 *You meet a former colleague, who recently went to work for another company. What do you say?*
>
> (SIX SECONDS)

(Arels Examination in Spoken English and Comprehension, Higher Level)

Possible responses:
7 This is where I get off. It's been very nice talking to you. Goodbye.
8 Sorry, but I'll have to be going. I've got an appointment in ten minutes. See you at lunchtime. OK?
9 Hi, Paul. How are you getting on with the new company?

2 Give pairs the first worksheet. Student A reads out a situation and student B responds. Student B must not look at the text until after he or she has responded. They continue until they have practised with all the remaining situations.

3 Put the class into groups of four. Explain that they are going to be given some responses and should write suitable situations. Give each group a set of four responses. For example:

- Good evening. I'm calling about the ad in the paper for a second-hand PC. Can you tell me a bit more about it, please?
- Not for me thanks. I've been trying to give them up ever since I saw that TV programme.
- Well, the first thing I saw was a man running away from the shop with what looked like a knife in his hand.
- Hi, it's me. I'll try ringing again in the morning but if you come in you can call me back at any time up to eleven tonight. Bye.

5 Allow a few minutes for students to discuss these and to write a situation for each on a separate piece of paper.

6 Students pass the situations to another group, who take it in turns to read them out to the rest of the group and elicit responses.

VARIATION

At stage 6, when a student receives a situation on a piece of paper he or she responds to the situation instead of reading it out. The other three listen and try to guess what the situation is.

6.12 From role-card to essay

LEVEL

Intermediate and above

AIMS

To encourage group discussion; to practise writing instructions, listening for main points, and writing discursive (for and against) essays

TIME

90 minutes

PREPARATION

None

PROCEDURE

1 Groups of four decide on characters for a role-play in which the teacher will take part. For example:

- teacher/angry school director;
- rock star/ex-fan;
- US President/husband or wife;
- member of Royal Family/husband or wife;
- oral examiner/unsuccessful candidate.

2 Students write the instructions on role-cards: one for the teacher and another for themselves. Give help where necessary and allow time for students to think about what they are going to say.

3 The role-play takes place (5–10 minutes), with members of the group taking turns to speak. The rest of the class listen and note down the main arguments on both sides as an essay framework.

4 The next group gives its role-card to the teacher and stage 3 is repeated. The other groups follow.

5 Each student chooses one of the topics and writes up the essay for homework.

Example

ROLE-CARD A

You are representing the British/American Government abroad in a television current affairs programme for young people. People there believe that the US/Britain long ago used its military strength to take part of your country's territory or national heritage and should now return it. Argue your government's case on historical, legal, moral, and practical grounds. Propose solutions, including compromises. Answer all the interviewers' questions and do not get angry.

ROLE-CARD B

You are interviewing a representative of the British/American Government in a television current affairs programme for young people in your country. You believe that the US/Britain used its military strength to take part of your country's territory or national heritage and should now hand it back. Argue your country's case on historical, legal, moral, and practical grounds. Propose solutions but do not accept any offers of compromise. Make sure he or she answers all your questions.

Photocopiable © Oxford University Press

COMMENTS   This often works best as an end-of-term activity, when students have taken part in a lot of role-plays and worked with plenty of role-cards.

6.13 Candidates and examiners

LEVEL   **Upper-intermediate and above**

AIMS   **To encourage critical awareness of candidate performance and the interview procedure; to practise speaking skills and student–student error correction**

TIME   **60 minutes**

PREPARATION   1 Ensure the class have access to plenty of oral exam materials. A recorded sample interview would be useful.

PROCEDURE   1 Ask the class what they know about the exam interview.
2 Play the recording of a sample exam or do a model interview with a volunteer student. While they listen, the class compare with what they said at stage 1.

3 In pairs students practise examining each other using some of the materials you have prepared.

4 Put the class into groups of four, assigning the roles of examiner (interlocutor), examiner (assessor), and two candidates. Give the interviewing examiners some testing materials such as picture prompts, and tell the assessors to keep a note of the candidates' strengths and weaknesses. On the positive side these could be, for example, a good range of vocabulary, clear pronunciation, and a pleasant manner. Weak points might include language errors which impede communication, or simply not talking enough, but do remind the examiners to be tactful, especially with weaker students or those who lack confidence.

5 When the interview has ended, the candidates leave the examiners and talk to each other about how well they think they did—and also how it went in terms of organization, materials, questions, and attitude on the part of the examiners—just as they might, in fact, after the real exam. The examiners, meanwhile, compare impressions of the candidates.

6 The groups re-form. Examiners and candidates say what they think about each other's performance, comment on their own difficulties, and suggest ways of improving both in the future.

7 Groups report back to the class—not about individuals but on difficulties and possible solutions.

VARIATION   At stage 5, an examiners' meeting is held for all those who conducted and assessed the interviews. They identify the most common problems overall and put forward recommendations for both candidates and examiners in future interviews. The candidates themselves, meanwhile, get together to talk about their feelings about their own performance, and possibly suggest improvements in the way the orals are conducted. A class discussion between the two sides follows.

COMMENTS

This activity helps to demystify the interview by enabling students to experience and discuss the difficulties faced not only by candidates but also by examiners, for example how to relax candidates, how to get them to talk more so that a fair assessment can be made, and how to avoid one candidate dominating the other. It also gives valuable language skills practice. Before doing this activity, however, thought should be given as to whether some students may feel uncomfortable exchanging opinions about each other. If for personal or cultural reasons this is the case, omit stages 4–6.

6.14 Inter-class examining

LEVEL

Lower-intermediate and above, plus a higher level class

AIMS

To focus on interview materials, assessment scales, and procedure; to develop speaking skills; to appreciate the examiner's task

TIME

Practice 60 minutes, activity 60 minutes, follow-up 15 minutes

PREPARATION

1 This activity requires the participation of two exam classes of different levels, so arrangements need to be made with another teacher to bring them together for an hour. This is, of course, more feasible if the classes coincide or at least overlap on the timetable. Copies of materials similar to those used in both exams will be required.

2 In a lesson—or series of lessons—before the day the classes are brought together, the higher-level students practise interviewing one another using materials, marking scales, and mark sheets like those used in their exam. Monitor their interviews and suggest improvements in the way they conduct them. The less advanced class work in small groups, asking each other questions about pictures, texts, or other materials similar to those in the exam they will be taking.

3 The higher-level class are given scales and mark sheets for the lower-level exam, together with enough materials to conduct at least three interviews. They are asked to study them carefully. Copies of the exam board's instructions for oral examiners can also be very useful, if they are available.

PROCEDURE

1 Bring both classes together in a large room, assigning the role of 'examiners' to the higher-level students and 'candidates' to the less advanced ones. Spread out the tables and arrange the chairs according to the seating format of the lower-level exam.

2 Allocate a candidate to each examiner (or whatever the number of candidates and examiners that normally take part in the exam). If there are more students in one class than the other, give the stronger examiners an extra candidate or the weaker ones an 'assessor' to help them. Similar changes can be made for group interviews.

3 Complete exam-style interviews take place and marks are awarded. To keep a check on standards, you may wish to sit in and observe some interviews as a 'supervisor'—as sometimes happens in actual oral exams.

4 After about 20 minutes (or however long the interview plus paperwork usually takes in the real exam) the supervisors collect the mark sheets and the candidates move to the tables of other examiners, who use a different set of testing materials with them.

5 Stages 3 and 4 are repeated at least twice.

6 Compare the assessments with your own formal and informal assessments from earlier lessons. If you feel the student examiners have made reasonably accurate assessments, tell the candidates their marks.

FOLLOW-UP

In the next lesson, give feedback based on your observations as a supervisor—and ask the class what they learnt from the experience. Ask the higher-level students if they would act differently as candidates after seeing the interview from the examiners' perspective. Might they be more forthcoming? More concerned with fluency than accuracy? Less intimidated by the situation? Ask the lower-level students what differences they expect in the real exam and tell them if there are any significant ones. If you feel the marks awarded concur with your own assessments, tell the students the results. Make peer interviewing a regular classroom activity as the exam approaches.

COMMENTS

This activity works particularly well with younger students. As a rule very little supervision is needed, although occasionally it is advisable to check that the 'examiners' are not being over-strict with the 'candidates'.

Answers

6.1 1D   2F   3G   4L   5J   6H   7K   8E   9A
       10C   11B   12I

6.6 1c   2b   3d   4e   5a

Examinations

Cambridge Key English Test (KET)

Board: University of Cambridge Local Examinations Syndicate (UCLES), 1 Hills Rd, Cambridge CB1 2EU, UK.
Level: Beginner.
Recognition: Recognized as Council of Europe Waystage level.
Availability: Worldwide. 5 times per year.
Papers: Reading/Writing, Listening, Speaking.

Cambridge Preliminary English Test (PET)

Board: UCLES.
Level: Elementary.
Recognition: Recognized as Council of Europe Threshold level.
Availability: Worldwide. 5 times per year.
Papers: Reading, Writing, Listening, Speaking.

Cambridge First Certificate in English (FCE), Revised 1996

Board: UCLES.
Level: Intermediate.
Recognition: Recognized in commerce, industry, and education as proof of ability at this level.
Availability: Worldwide. June and December.
Papers: Reading, Writing, Use of English, Listening, Speaking.

Cambridge Certificate in Advanced English (CAE)

Board: UCLES.
Level: Advanced.
Recognition: Pass recognized as an entrance requirement by British universities.
Availability: Worldwide. June and December.
Papers: Reading, Writing, English in Use, Listening, Speaking.

Cambridge Certificate of Proficiency in English (CPE)

Board: UCLES.

Level: Advanced.

Recognition: Pass for university entry, business, and professional purposes in Britain and elsewhere. Language qualification for teaching English in some countries.

Availability: Worldwide. June and December.

Papers: Reading Comprehension, Composition, Use of English, Listening Comprehension, Interview.

Cambridge Certificates in Communication Skills in English (CCSE)

Board: UCLES

Levels: Elementary to Advanced.

Availability: Worldwide. June and November.

Papers: Reading, Writing, Listening, Oral Interaction. Can be taken separately and at different levels. Test what candidates can do, rather than penalize them for what they cannot do.

International English Language Testing System (IELTS)

Board: British Council/UCLES/IDP Education Australia, GPO Box 2006, Canberra, ACT 2601, Australia.

Level: Advanced

Recognition: Bands 5.5 to 7 for British university entry. Recognized for academic and professional purposes outside the UK.

Availability: Worldwide. No set dates.

Papers: Listening, Academic Reading or General Training Reading, Academic Writing or General Training Writing, Speaking.

Test of English as a Foreign Language (TOEFL®), Revised 1995

Board: Educational Testing Service, TOEFL, PO Box 6155, Princeton, New Jersey 08541–6155, USA.

Level: Advanced.

Recognition: Scores 500–580 for university entry in the USA, Canada, the UK and elsewhere (evidence of spoken/written English may also be required). Scores valid two years.

Availability: Worldwide. Every month.

Papers: Listening Comprehension, Structure and Written Expression, Reading Comprehension. Optional Test of Written English (TWE): Essay. Optional Test of Spoken English (TSE): Oral (recorded).

Extensive revisions expected in 2000.

Oxford-Arels Preliminary Examination

Board: University of Oxford Delegacy of Local Examinations/Arels Examinations Trust, Ewert Place, Summertown, Oxford OX2 7BZ, UK.

Level: Elementary.

Recognition: Recognized as Council of Europe Waystage level.

Availability: Worldwide. March, May, November.

Papers: Writing, Reading and Writing (Oxford). Oral, recorded (Arels). Also Junior counterpart for both.

Oxford-Arels Higher Examination

Board: University of Oxford Delegacy of Local Examinations/ Arels Examinations Trust.

Level: Upper-intermediate/Advanced.

Recognition: Credit in written and Pass in spoken for British university entry.

Availability: Worldwide. March, May, November.

Papers: Writing, Reading and Writing (Oxford). Oral, recorded (Arels).

Grade Examinations in Spoken English for Speakers of Other Languages

Board: Trinity College London, 16 Park Crescent, London W1N 4AP, UK.

Levels: Initial (Grade 1) to Advanced level (Grade 12).

Recognition: Grades 10–12 for British university entry.

Availability: Worldwide. Examiners visit on demand.

Papers: Oral interview. Also Written English (Intermediate).

Michigan English Language Assessment Battery (MELAB)

Board: University of Michigan English Language Institute, Testing and Certification Division, Ann Arbor, Michigan 48109–1057, USA.

Level: Advanced.

Recognition: Scores 75–90 for university entry in the USA and Canada. Scores valid two years.

Availability: Worldwide (individually on demand).

Papers: Composition, Listening, Grammar/Cloze/Vocabulary/Reading. Optional Oral.

IB English as a Second Language

Board: International Baccalaureate Organisation, Route des Morillons 15, CH-1218 Grand-Saconnex, Geneva, Switzerland.

Level: Advanced.

Recognition: 'Higher' for university entry in many countries.

Availability: Worldwide. May. Also November in the southern hemisphere.

Papers: Linguistic tests, Commentary and essay, Oral examination.

Examinations in Languages for International Communication (ELIC)

Board: Institute of Linguists, 24a Highbury Grove, London N5 2EA, UK.

Levels: Preliminary, General, Advanced, Intermediate Diploma, Diploma.

Recognition: Advanced for British higher education entry. Diploma degree equivalent.

Availability: Worldwide. May.

Papers: Reading, Listening, Speaking (lower levels). Modular (higher levels).

PEI English for Speakers of Other Languages (ESOL)

Board: Pitman Examination Institute, Godalming, Surrey GU7 1UU, UK.

Levels: Basic, Elementary, Intermediate, Higher Intermediate, Advanced.

Recognition: Advanced and (in some cases) Higher Intermediate for British university entry, professional bodies, and commerce.

Availability: Worldwide. Dates depend on local centres.

Papers: Listening, English Usage, Reading, Reading and Writing, Writing. Also PEI ESOL for Young Learners and Spoken ESOL.

Certificate of Attainment in English

Board: London Examinations International, 32 Russell Square, London WC1B 5DN, UK.

Levels: Beginners (Level 1) to Advanced (Level 6).

Recognition: Higher levels facilitate admission to English-speaking universities.

Availability: Worldwide. March, May, July, September, December.

Papers: 6 parts, varying according to level and whether done in language laboratory.

English as an Acquired Language

Board: English Speaking Board (International), 26a Princes Street, Southport PR8 1EQ, UK.

Levels: Foundation 1–3, Intermediate 1–3, Advanced 1–3. Higher Certificate.

Recognition: Recognized by British SEAC and DFC.

Availability: Worldwide. Assessments on demand.

Papers: Oral assessment.

ICC Certificate in English

Board: International Certificate Conference, Holzhausen str. 21, D6000 Frankfurt 1, Germany.

Levels: Elementary (Stage 1), Lower-intermediate (Certificate), Intermediate (Stage 3).

Recognition: Recognized in member states of the ICC (Western Europe).

Availability: Western Europe. On demand.

Papers: Oral, Writing, Knowledge of the English Language (Stage 3).

Bibliography

Further information on examinations

British Council. 1994. *English Language Entrance Requirements.*
London: British Council.
Carroll, B.J. and **R. West.** 1989. *The ESU Framework: Performance
Scales for English Language Examinations.* London: Longman.
Davies, S. and **R. West.** 1989. *The Longman Guide to English
Language Examinations.* London: Longman.

Sources of useful material

The examination boards listed on pages 159–63 will all supply past
papers or sample tests, and for many of the exams there is a range of
coursebooks, practice tests, and supplementary materials which is too
extensive to list here. The following, however, contain material which is
particularly suitable for use in conjunction with this book.

Campbell, C. and **H. Kryszewska.** 1996. *Learner-based Teaching.*
Oxford: Oxford University Press.
Cole, L. and **C. Jones.** 1989. *Teaching the First Certificate in English.*
London: Phoenix. Explains how examiners assess and suggests many
practical classroom ideas using exam materials.
Folse, K. 1995. *Intermediate TOEFL: Test Practice.* University of
Michigan Press. Simpler language for students currently scoring
410–500. Tapescripts.
Fried-Booth, D. L. 1996. *PET Practice Tests.* Oxford: Oxford
University Press. With Answers edition. Contains transcripts; sample
answers to Writing Part 3, with assessment criteria and marks; and a
sample speaking test. Photocopiable answer sheets.
Gairns, R. and **G. Workman.** 1987. *Teaching Exam Classes.* London:
International House. Useful ideas for the teacher on many aspects of
exam class teaching.
Gear, J. 1994. *Cambridge Preparation for the TOEFL Test.* Cambridge:
Cambridge University Press. Essays with assessment.
Greenwood, J. 1988. *Class Readers.* Oxford: Oxford University Press.
Harris, M. and **P. McCann.** 1994. *Assessment.* Oxford: Heinemann.
Practical ideas for learner self-assessment.
Harrison, M. and **R. Kerr.** 1994. *CAE Practice Tests.* Oxford: Oxford
University Press. Essays with assessment.
Lukey Coutsocostas, K. and **D. Dalmaris.** 1995. *First Certificate
Practice Tests.* London: Phoenix. Analysis of common distractors and
explanations of marking schemes.

May, P. 1990, 1992. *The Complete Proficiency Practice Tests 1 & 2.* Oxford: Heinemann. Essays, open-ended questions, summaries, and recorded interviews with examiners' assessment.

McCallum, G. P. 1995. *Michigan Proficiency Practice Tests.* London: Nelson. Includes a description of the exam plus advice and guidance.

MELAB. 1995. *MELAB Information Bulletin and Registration Form.* Ann Arbor: University of Michigan. Description of the Michigan exam with advice. Rating scales for the composition and oral.

Morgan, J. and **M. Rinvolucri.** 1986. *Vocabulary.* Oxford: Oxford University Press.

Nolasco, R. 1987. *Success at First Certificate: the interview.* Oxford: Oxford University Press. Video guide to the stages of the oral and marking criteria with transcript.

Swan, H.A. 1989. *Oxford Higher Practice Book.* London: Nelson. Information about the marking system; specimen papers.

Swan, M. and **B. Smith.** 1987. *Learner English.* Cambridge: Cambridge University Press. Guide to first language interference problems of students.

TOEFL. 1995a. *Test Preparation Kit.* New Jersey: Educational Testing Service. Listening tapescripts. Answers and scoring information. Sample essays for TWE.

TOEFL. 1995b. *TOEFL Sample Test, Fifth Edition.* New Jersey: Educational Testing Service. Includes a description of the test, how to prepare for it, and how to take it.

UCLES. 1984 onwards. *Cambridge First Certificate Examination Practice, Cambridge Proficiency Examination Practice* series. Cambridge: Cambridge University Press. Recordings from past papers, with transcripts, in teacher's books. Some sample essays.

UCLES. 1994. *First Certificate in English Handbook.* Cambridge: UCLES. Sample materials plus candidate scripts with examiners' comments/grades. Exam listening transcripts. Similar handbooks also available for other UCLES exams.

UCLES. 1995a. *IELTS Specimen Materials with Cassette.* Cambridge: UCLES. Produced according to UCLES' question paper production cycle.

UCLES. 1995b. *Specifications and Sample Papers for the Revised FCE Examination, Second Edition.* Cambridge: UCLES. The changes explained, with transcripts, sample scripts, and information about the marking.

UCLES and **L. Hashemi.** 1991. *Cambridge First Certificate Examination Practice 2, Self-Study Edition.* Listening transcript with guide to clues. Focus on reading comprehension distractors. Recorded interview with transcript and comments. For pre-1996 syllabus but still useful.

Ward, A. 1994. *PET Preparation and Practice.* Oxford: Oxford University Press. Answers for writing tasks with assessment.

Sources of examples

Lawlor, M. 1993. 'Teaching Languages Holistically.' *The Linguist* 32/3: 70.

Le Carré, J. 1987. *A Perfect Spy.* London: Coronet.

Moore, G. 1981. 'Untilled field.' in B. Kielly (ed.): *The Penguin Book of Irish Short Stories.* Harmondsworth, London: Penguin.

Index of tasks

(In addition to task names, see under general headings: Extended reading, etc.)

Other titles in the Resource Books for Teachers series

Beginners, by Peter Grundy—over 100 original, communicative activities for teaching both absolute and 'false' beginners, including those who do not know the Latin alphabet. (ISBN 0 19 437200 6)

CALL, by David Hardisty and Scott Windeatt—a bank of practical activities, based on communicative methodology, which makes use of a variety of computer programs. (ISBN 0 19 437105 0)

Class Readers, by Jean Greenwood—practical advice and activities to develop extensive and intensive reading skills, listening activities, oral tasks, and perceptive skills. (ISBN 0 19 437103 4)

Classroom Dynamics, by Jill Hadfield—a practical book to help teachers maintain a good working relationship with their classes, and so promote effective learning. (ISBN 0 19 437096 8)

Conversation, by Rob Nolasco and Lois Arthur—more than 80 activities which develop students' ability to speak confidently and fluently. (ISBN 0 19 437096 8)

Cultural Awareness, by Barry Tomalin and Susan Stempleski—activities to challenge stereotypes, using cultural issues as a rich resource for language practice. (ISBN 0 19 437194 8)

Drama, by Charlyn Wessels—first-hand, practical advice on using drama to teach spoken communication skills and literature, and to make language learning more creative and enjoyable. (ISBN 0 19 437097 6)

Grammar Dictation, by Ruth Wajnryb—also known as 'dictogloss', this technique improves students' understanding and use of grammar by reconstructing texts. (ISBN 0 19 437097 6)

Learner-based Teaching, by Colin Campbell and Hanna Kryszewska—over 70 language practice activities which unlock the wealth of knowledge that learners bring to the classroom. (ISBN 0 19 437163 8)

Letters, by Nicky Burbidge, Peta Gray, Sheila Levy, and Mario Rinvolucri—demonstrates the rich possibilities of letters for language and cultural study. Contains numerous photocopiables and a section on email. (ISBN 0 19 442149 X)

Literature, by Alan Maley and Alan Duff—an innovatory book on using literature for language practice. (ISBN 0 19 437094 1)

Music and Song, by Tim Murphey—shows teachers how 'tuning in' to their students' musical tastes can increase motivation and tap a rich vein of resources. (ISBN 0 19 437055 0)

Newspapers, by Peter Grundy—creative and original ideas for making effective use of newspapers in lessons. (ISBN 0 19 437192 6)

Project Work, by Diana L. Fried-Booth—practical resources to bridge the gap between the classroom and the outside world. (ISBN 0 19 437092 5)

Pronunciation, by Clement Laroy—imaginative activities to build confidence and improve all aspects of pronunciation. (ISBN 0 19 437089 9)

Role Play, by Gillian Porter Ladousse—from highly controlled conversations to improvised drama, and from simple dialogues to complex scenarios. (ISBN 0 19 437095 X)

Self-Access, by Susan Sheerin—helps teachers with the practicalities of setting up and managing self-access study facilities. (ISBN 0 19 437099 2)

Storytelling with Children, by Andrew Wright—thirty stories plus hundreds of exciting ideas for using any story to teach English to children aged 7 to 14. (ISBN 0 19 437202 2)

Translation, by Alan Duff—provides a wide variety of translation activities from many different subject areas. (ISBN 0 19 437104 2)

Video, by Richard Cooper, Mike Lavery, and Mario Rinvolucri—video watching and making tasks involving the language of perception, observation, and argumentation. (ISBN 0 19 437192 6)

Vocabulary, by John Morgan and Mario Rinvolucri—a wide variety of communicative activities for teaching new words to learners of any foreign language. (ISBN 437091 7)

Writing, by Tricia Hedge—presents a wide range of writing tasks to improve learners' 'authoring' and 'crafting' skills, as well as guidance on student difficulties with writing. (ISBN 0 19 437098 4)

Young Learners, by Sarah Phillips—advice, ideas, and materials for a wide variety of language activities, including arts and crafts, games, storytelling, poems, and songs. (ISBN 0 19 437 195 6)